MISTY
OUR MOMENTARY
CHILD

MISTY

OUR MOMENTARY CHILD

A Mother's Journey
Through Sorrow to Healing

Carole Gift Page

H

L.³

CROSSWAY BOOKS • WESTCHESTER, ILLINOIS
A DIVISION OF GOOD NEWS PUBLISHERS

J

First printing, 1987

Printed in the United States of America

Library of Congress Catalog Card Number 87-70455

ISBN 0-89107-450-3

Cover calligraphy by Paul Higdon
Cover illustration by Floyd E. Hosmer.
  Copyright © 1987 by Floyd E. Hosmer.
Book design by K. L. Mulder

DEDICATION

To my husband Bill
And to our four children
here—and there

Kimberle Carole Page
David Aldon Page
Heather Gift Page
Misty Lynne Page

PROLOGUE

A FEW YEARS AGO I WAS juggling four careers—wife, mother, freelance writer, and creative writing instructor at Biola University. It was the life I'd always wanted. My husband, Bill, was incredibly supportive; my nine-year-old son David and eleven-year-old daughter Kim were finally at an age that allowed me some freedom to pursue my own career goals.

Then, one December morning as I sat reading the current issue of *Christianity Today*, my life changed course. In an article on abortion, Dr. C. Everett Koop (presently Surgeon General of the United States) pointed out that the intrauterine device used for birth control can, in fact, cause abortion. He noted that the IUD acts after the egg is fertilized, preventing implantation on the uterus wall. Thus, the IUD may actually cast off a fertilized egg that would have become a baby.

As the import of Dr. Koop's words gripped me, I felt a chilling wave of shock. I had used an IUD for ten years and had never been warned that conception could take place. The idea that conception and abortion could have occurred within my body without my knowledge or approval was abhorrent to me.

As I put the magazine aside, I knew the IUD was

no longer an acceptable option for me. But if not the IUD, then what? Every birth control method I considered had serious drawbacks. Yet Bill and I couldn't risk having more children.

Or could we? It was a new, disconcerting thought. Did God want us to have more children? For ten years I had assumed He didn't. Our budget was already stretched to the limits with two. And with our second child we had discovered an ABO blood incompatibility, similar to the RH factor, that could threaten future children. Besides, pregnancy carried added risks for a woman over thirty-five.

And there was my career to think of. I considered my writing a God-given ministry, a chance to reach people around the world for Christ while remaining in my own home. Surely it was time for my career to take priority.

But God spoke to me in a still, small voice and said, *I want you to be willing to have another child. Be willing to put home and family before your career. I have new things to teach you in your relationship with Me.*

And so, after much prayer and soul-searching, I said, "Yes, Lord, I am willing."

By the following November I was pregnant. God had so prepared my heart—and Bill's—that we were eager for this third child. When friends reacted with surprise and made little jokes about our "accident," I wanted to share with them the long, careful process of growth and acceptance God had worked in our lives. Our baby was no accident; rather, this was a step of faith and obedience to God's special plan for our family.

In July our beautiful little daughter Heather was born, perfect in every detail. Bill participated in her natural birth, and we both praised God for the miracle of new life. As I settled into the almost forgotten routine of new motherhood—nursing, diapering, singing lullabies, and walking the floor at midnight—I reflected with pleasure that Bill and I had followed God's directive and the Lord had blessed us far beyond what we had hoped.

But as Heather grew quickly from an infant to a toddler, a strange stirring started within me. I tried to ignore it, but the feeling wouldn't be argued or bluffed or bullied away. God seemed to be saying, *I want you to be willing to have still another child. I have more things to teach you.*

"Lord, You can't mean it!" I wanted to exclaim. "At my age? What will people say? We got by with one 'accident,' but *two*? People will think we're crazy! *I'll* think we're crazy! And what will Bill say? One baby was a big step of faith. Are You really asking us to take that same giant step all over again?"

I'm asking only that you be willing. Leave the rest with Me.

Again I chose to believe God, to trust Him with my future.

Bill responded with surprising good nature when I told him I felt we should use no precautions for just a few months. We both agreed that, because of my age, if God really wanted us to have another child He would have to act promptly.

He did.

I got pregnant that very first month. Heather was only ten months old, still a baby herself.

After the initial shock, Bill and I both felt as excited about this new pregnancy as we had been over Heather's birth. I loved this unseen baby with the same fierce mother-hen protectiveness that I felt for my other three children.

The next six months were the smoothest, most trouble-free of any of my pregnancies. I suffered little morning sickness or exhaustion. My mind was at its most creative as I swiftly completed half a novel in a few months' time. I felt wonderful, exuberant, buoyed with energy.

Then, one unforgettable day in November, God

began to unfold, slowly and carefully, with utmost love, His plan for our family—the hard, bitter journey we would have to take in the months to come.

Our Jesus would not require us to travel this difficult road alone. He would go before us all the way.

Still, walk it we must.

A BEGINNING

I begin a journey.
Unplanned.
Quixotic.
Hard.
Maddening.
Mystifying.
I ask, How did I get on this roller-coaster?
How do I get off?
I ask, Am I normal?
Am I crazy?
How do I cope?
How have others coped?
I need a road map, a guidebook,
someone to point the way.
I hunger for someone to share the pain,
to assure me I won't always feel
lost, baffled, strung out, angry, helpless.
Like a drowning victim, I clutch for God.
He is there.
Now I know: The grief is bearable.
I will survive.
I reach out to you—

travelers on this road with me.
I embrace you
love you.
I long to touch your hurting heart
and whisper, You are not alone.
You who mourn
let me hold you in my arms
and croon a mother's lullaby.
You who weep
listen
for the Father's soothing cradlesong.
Walk hand in hand with me
and together we'll be strong.
Learn with me:
Joy can come again
even
when your baby dies.

MISTY, OUR MOMENTARY CHILD

Children are not supposed to die.
They are too new
their faces gleaming
with suns of astonishment.
They run
their voices shrill and confident
day in, day out.
They live forever.
But you, my child,
die all too soon—
the day before tomorrow.
In your face
your destiny written—
ice-smooth cheeks
melting with the moons
and shadowed eyes
already old
that have not begun
to see the world.
Your world was to have been this room
with cartoon animals on the walls
and arrows of treetops

MISTY

beyond these saffron curtains
holding back wings of splintered sunlight.

Misty, our momentary child,
shattering our defenses with a sigh—
bittersweet babysong—
you fled your cradle-womb
too soon.
Your life hard-won
journey just begun,
you stayed an hour
or more,
precious pause
between two worlds
that we might cuddle
and adore you.
Then
while we wept
you crept
soundlessly
on angel palms
into your Father's arms.

MONDAY, NOVEMBER 23

ELEVEN A.M. A routine office visit to my obstetrician. During the examination Dr. Natter notices that my uterus is unusually large for the sixth month of pregnancy. He sends me to the hospital for an ultrasound with the tantalizing, terrifying observation, "You may be expecting twins."

I'm incredulous. *Twins? Me? A woman over thirty-five with a full-time writing career, lecturing commitments, and a teenager, preteen, and toddler at home?*

I walk down the hospital corridor, my feet not quite touching the floor, my heart racing with panic and visions and rapture.

Twins? Wonderful! Oh, God, no, You wouldn't, would You? Yes, please, who would believe it!

For the sonogram I must drink huge quantities of water. Discomfort is too mild a word for what I feel now. I am a walking water balloon, about to burst.

Besides the misery of a full bladder, I have to endure the shock of cold oil smeared repeatedly over my bare belly. As the technician guides her transducer-paddle back and forth over my skin, eerie black and white images create a fetal outline on the ultrasound screen.

My baby—a puzzle, an abstract painting in assorted grays, an undulating test pattern, TV performer. I can't read you, guess you. My cherished mystery. And you may be two!

The technician is closemouthed, button-lipped as she works. I try to fish for information without really appearing to do so. I tell her the doctor said there might be twins.

"I see only one baby," she tells me.

Oh.

If not twins, then what? A problem? Women in their late thirties sometimes have Mongoloid children.

"What about the size of the baby's head?" I venture.

"Looks about right," she says. But that is all she will say. And there is something in her expression, something in what she is not saying that makes me wary. All my inflated wonder and joy and incredulity have shrunken into a hard, small knot of concern. Wordless. Unarticulated. A foreign matter in my skull.

I go home silenced by questions. Okay, not twins. Something else. Something *wrong?* Oh, God, what?

TUESDAY, NOVEMBER 24

BARELY SUPPRESSING my anxiety, I telephone Dr. Natter for the results of the sonogram. His voice is subdued, but his words drill my mind like bullets. "It looks like there's a problem with the baby, Carole."

My breath catches. "What is it?"

"Hydrocephalus."

I wrack my brain for comprehension. "You mean Down's syndrome?"

"No. Water on the brain."

"What does that mean?"

Dr. Natter's voice remains calm, perfectly modulated. "There's an abnormal fluid buildup putting pressure on the brain, supplanting brain tissue. If not corrected, it will cause brain damage . . . even death."

He hastens to explain that after birth, a shunt or

tube can be surgically placed in the baby's head to drain the fluids. *If it's not too late. If the damage hasn't already been done.*

My mind summons grotesque images of the mal-formed children my good writer friend Till Fell, also a nurse, used to care for. How she ached with compassion as she cradled and prayed over those helpless babies with balloon heads, tagged by some as "vegetables," with no hope, no promise, waiting to die.

God, not my baby, please! That is the ultimate night-mare.

WEDNESDAY, NOVEMBER 25

A HECTIC DAY. ON THE PHONE trying to talk to the doctor. He never calls back.

I need more information. I need to know what's hap-pening to my baby!

I'm helping Bill and our son pack for their long-planned trip to Mexico. Midnight flight to Mexico City. Bill saying, "Should I go?"

Me saying, with more bravado than I feel, "Yes, go. You and David need this time together."

Last-minute packing. Confusion. Kentucky Chick-en for dinner. (Who's hungry?) Bill and David out the door in a rush of kisses and good-byes.

Don't miss your plane! Yes, I'll be fine. Just go!

Now: Kim, Heather, and I alone for Thanksgiving weekend.

Me: Exhausted. Alone.

Why didn't the doctor call?

What about my baby?

THURSDAY, NOVEMBER 26

THANKSGIVING DAY. Seven-thirty A.M.

I am wide awake, my mind whirling. I lie in bed, my hand resting on my bulging abdomen.

Are you awake, baby? Where are the ripples of you, the sudden pokes and jabs, the gentle stirrings? Yes, there you are. Awake, like me. We two together. And God with us.

I talk to you, baby.

I talk to You, God.

Silently.

Beyond words. We are in this together, we three.

There is something I must do. The idea presses upon me. My first instinct always: To clarify life with words. To find the meaning. I must get up and put my thoughts and prayers down in a journal. I want a record of these days, something to look back on when the days get even harder.

First I stop by the next bedroom. Kim and Heather are still asleep. Heather, sixteen months old, lies on her stomach, her legs drawn up under her, turtle-fashion, her little rump in the air—the very position she assumed when the doctor placed her on my chest after birth. She leisurely sucks her index finger and clutches her favorite red-checkered blanket, my sweet, tawny-haired imp.

Kim, my graceful thirteen-year-old, is curled like a delicate flower, her long, slender legs folded against her chest. My two girls. I feel awe, watching them.

While they sleep I begin this journal. I pause only to wonder what Bill and David are doing this morning. Sightseeing in Mexico City? Climbing the pyramids? Anticipating their flight to Acapulco and return cruise on the *S. S. Oriana?*

It's later now. Kim is up, pajama-clad, sitting cross-legged on the rug, watching the Thanksgiving Day parade on TV. The bright colors and motion are a blur to me. I am numb. I feel no joy. In a moment of frustration I blurt, "Thanksgiving? I'd like to bury the day under a rock!"

I mean it, but I don't mean it. These last few days have been shattering, exhausting. They have turned everything around, brought me up short, and I recognize—reluctantly—that they are only the beginning.

What I have always most feared stares me stark in the face: the death or severe brain damage of my child.

I have carried this unborn baby for six months. He is mine; he moves and wiggles and hiccups and keeps me company. He is my child, full of promise and hopes and dreams; limitless possibilities. God chose this particular baby to be conceived, to come into existence. I must believe God has a reason and a purpose for his life even now, however brief or troubled it may be.

I pray constantly. Consciously. Unconsciously. I pray now, with an urgency I haven't felt in weeks.

Father.
My Father.
Heavenly Father. Where are the words I need to say? The words to make You real?

Listen, Father. I know You. I know who You are. I know You do nothing capriciously. You love me . . . and my baby. Work all things out in the days ahead for our good. And Yours.

I ask for Your strength, Jesus. Gethsemane strength. Calvary strength. Mine is so flimsy, so faltering in the face of adversity. Yours is eternal, immovable, and always available. Share it with Bill and me, Lord, even when we are too weak, too human, or too blind to reach out for it.

FRIDAY, NOVEMBER 27

MY SECOND ULTRASOUND TODAY. My friend Vicki Wilhite drives me to the medical center through chill, slanting rain. Again I must drink ghastly quantities of fluid. I carry a plastic pitcher of iced tea which I sip through a straw while Vicki drives.

At the hospital I wait one and a half hours for my test. The ultrasound itself takes another hour and a half. The technicians bring in three different machines to take their pictures.

I watch the screen intently, observe the globular jelly shapes swell and recede—the thrusting, twisting movements of my tiny inhabitant, my gyrator-gymnast.

Those ghostly patterns—liquid flashes of quicksilver and ectoplasm—tell my baby's fate. If only I could decipher them!

I want to ask a dozen questions, convince the technicians I already know there's trouble. They don't have to maintain their stoical silence on my account. I want honesty, facts, answers. I want to know what Baby and I are up against.

But medical protocol puts openness and communication at a premium. I must wait for the radiologist to unravel the mystery.

He, too, is reluctant to say much. He confirms only that the baby has hydrocephalus.

How I was praying he would say it's all a mistake, the baby's fine!

"How bad is it?" I ask.

His reply is restrained. "There's a moderate amount of fluid on the baby's brain. I've seen women in here whose babies were worse." He doesn't add that he's seen them better as well.

He explains a possible surgical procedure recently performed on a few hydrocephalic fetuses. He defines the procedure as "experimental," bringing all sorts of questionable images to mind. He admits, too, that the surgery would pose a risk to the baby.

But my baby is already under great risk.

SATURDAY, NOVEMBER 28

I'M READING IN THE PSALMS. Psalm 71:6 catches my attention: "By thee have I been held up from the womb; thou art he who took me out of my mother; my praise shall be continually of thee."

I am reminded that God is in control of our lives

even before we leave the womb. I praise Him for that reassurance.

A thought comes to me: Better is a time of trial with God's presence than a time of plenty without Him. This idea has proved itself to me these past few days as I've faced again the fact of my total dependency on God. It's a fact I know well. Yet I tend to ignore the truth of it. I go my way and fret through daily irritations that pull me down and drain my spiritual energy.

For weeks I've felt on the verge of depression over the constant pressures of caring for a very active toddler, of feeling the physical weight and minor complaints of pregnancy, of trying to keep up with household obligations and family care, and in all of the busy routine, trying to find a moment or two to write.

Oddly enough, those pressures were taking a greater toll on me than this present crisis—although I realize I am still on the threshold of this unpredictable situation.

Perhaps before, I wasn't casting all my cares on the Lord because the cares were too random, diverse, or nebulous to be pinpointed and dealt with effectively. Or maybe it is simply true that the routine pressures are more difficult to confront than the unexpected, infrequent crises.

SUNDAY, NOVEMBER 29

A QUIET, SUNNY MORNING after several days of pouring rain.

This week without Bill hasn't been as difficult as I expected. I surprise myself. I haven't felt regret or resentment, loneliness or depression. These days with Kim and Heather have been peaceful, orderly, even relaxing; times of special closeness between Kim and me—baking pies together, rubbing each other's back, playing Yahtzee, listening to Christmas music on the stereo.

Are these the days of peace before the storm?

I know my mind hasn't really assimilated what we are facing or what the prospects might be for our baby. If I grasped the full impact of it, perhaps I could not even cope. The mind provides its own balm of disbelief.

I wonder how well I'll trust God in the days ahead. I know how weak I am. I gravitate toward comfort and ease; I shun pain. If I cope, it is only because God is providing the strength.

Lord, I depend on You, upon Your Spirit, to break through the narrow strictures, the arid, stifling, self-imposed walls of my own will. I believe that all You bring into my life is for the purpose of creating Your character in me, of carving Your image upon my spirit to make me the person You want me to be.

Let Your Spirit short-circuit my "natural man" reactions. Rewire me with Your own godly responses. I know when the power is coming from You, Lord. It supersedes my own feelings. I sense the broad, vast, limitless potential of You within me.

MONDAY, NOVEMBER 30

I HAVE MISGIVINGS. I am sitting in the cramped, nondescript office of Dr. Peter Anzaldo, a high-risk OB specialist. I expected his office to be roomy and tastefully decorated, with an aura of understated luxury. Instead, the waiting room is like a closet; the chairs are crammed together, and nearly every seat is taken by young, blowzy-looking girls. I sit squeezed between two thickset women in faded, bulging jeans. They talk across me in loud, slangy voices about their high school days. I stare ahead, trying to quell a growing anxiety.

Can I trust this new doctor to help my baby? Will Bill join me in time for our consultation?

His ship should have docked at 8:00 A.M. Bill will

come here directly after going through customs and immigration. It's after 11 now. *I don't want to face this appointment alone.*

Bill arrives just one minute before the doctor summons me into his office. Tense and breathless, his sunburned forehead dotted with perspiration, Bill greets me with a quick hug and kiss. He smiles at me through his worry. We meet the doctor together, hand in hand.

Dr. Anzaldo is a personable young man of Mexican descent. Lean, wiry, and exuding an impression of perpetual energy, he moves with the agility of a gymnast. His face possesses a disarming, boyish animation; his black hair erupts from his head in unruly curls. As he greets us, his dark eyes meet ours directly. Bill and I sense genuine concern. We relax a little.

Dr. Anzaldo gets right to the point. "Your baby's condition is extremely serious," he says soberly. "He has just one-fifth of the brain tissue of a normal fetus." He pauses to allow his words to penetrate, then continues, "There is only a 25 to 50 percent chance of coming through this pregnancy with a relatively normal baby."

So. The odds are against you, little one. Is horror written on my face or only in my heart?

Dr. Anzaldo tells us about the experimental surgery the radiologist mentioned last Friday—a technique for draining the excess fluid from the baby's brain *in utero.* Only six of these operations have been performed in this country, making it even more experimental than I anticipated. The doctor explains that the surgery is not presently an option for me. It has been performed so far on women only four or five months into their pregnancies.

He outlines his plan of action for my baby: Twice a week for the next seven weeks I will undergo an ultrasound to determine whether the baby's condition has stabilized or deteriorated. If the fluid on the brain has not increased, I will go home and await my next appointment. But if there is any increase in fluid, Dr.

Anzaldo will admit me to the hospital for a cesarean section that very day. His goal is to balance the two dangers to my baby—the potential of profound brain damage from the hydrocephalus against the threat of death from immature lung and organ development.

It is a dreadful, incredible tightrope we are forced to walk. I must be prepared from week to week to enter the hospital for a C-section—major surgery! I won't know until each ultrasound whether that will be the day of my baby's birth. And only God knows the outcome.

Little baby, little baby, who are you to cause such an uproar, to turn our lives upside down? Six months ago you didn't even exist. I got along without you then. Why not now? Can I rationalize you away? If I lose you, I never quite had you anyway.

Idon'tknowyouIdon'tneedyouIdon'tloveyou.

I do.

Later: At home. Everyone in bed asleep. I sit in the living room in the dark listening to familiar hymns. I try to pray. I talk to my baby. The tears come fast and hard.

Child, I'm grieving.

Do you sense it?

Does the salt from my tears run through your veins and turn your nourishment bitter? You wriggle and cavort inside your secret womb-room as if the world were still a friendly place.

It's not.

I'm not.

I can't give you wholeness. I can't guarantee you life. I can't staunch the flow of that insidious fluid supplanting

*your brain tissue, robbing you of your chance to be normal.
What kind of mother am I? You've just begun and already I
can't help you.*

*Today I wanted to forget you. I wanted to reason you
out of existence. I wanted to spare myself the pain of being
tied to you.*

But I can't. We are one.

*I care deeply for you, little one. I love you sight
unseen, problems and all. And I will hurt desperately if I
lose you.*

*You may as well know the rest: I grieve for myself as
well as for you. I'll have no natural delivery, no normal
baby to nurse and cuddle. See? The losses accumulate, one
by one. I am awkward, unskilled at counting them.*

TUESDAY, DECEMBER 1

THE TRUTH ATTACHES ITSELF to me in barbed bits and
pieces—the reality of what I'm facing, of what my baby
is facing. I feel weary beyond words.

I am walking, eyes open, into the path of a racing
truck. It's going to hit; I know it's going to hit; and
there's not a thing I can do to prevent it. I am trembling
even now, thinking of it.

I struggle with the idea of asking for a miracle—a
sudden, inexplicable healing of my unborn child. I
know God can do it. But I can't presume to know His
will, His purpose for me and my baby.

God says, Make known to Me the desires of your
heart. So daily, constantly, I entreat Him for healing, a
miracle to make the fluid recede and normalcy to occur.
That is my prayer.

But even Jesus said, Not My will, but Thine be
done.

I know what I want. The deepest yearning of my
heart is for a healthy, normal baby. But if I must choose,
I want God's will even more.

THURSDAY, DECEMBER 3

ANOTHER SONOGRAM AT Memorial Hospital. Dr. Anzaldo is waiting for me in the ultrasound lab. There is something electric in his manner. "Where's hubby?" he asks, looking past me.

"Bill? He's working."

Dr. Anzaldo's smile wavers.

"I—I didn't know he was supposed to come too," I say hastily.

He recovers his grin. "That's all right. It's just that we need to sit down and talk."

We find a small, unoccupied office. He sits down behind the desk. I sit stiffly in a straight-back chair.

"I've conferred again with the specialists in San Francisco," he tells me. "They've decided to consider you as a candidate for their experimental surgical technique after all."

My mind races, trying to assimilate this new alternative. "Why did they change their minds?"

"With their present success rate, they feel the procedure warrants attempting it on older, viable fetuses," he replied. "So if today's ultrasound indicates that your baby's hydrocephalus has worsened, we will send you directly to San Francisco." His expression sobers as he adds, "Of course, if the baby's condition has deteriorated to a hopeless stage, we will do nothing."

I nod, fighting back shock. *Hopeless stage? My baby, would he actually write you off as hopeless just like that, without a fight?*

"I would like to do a blood test to check for possible spinal deformities," he continues. "And if you agree, an amniocentesis to rule out chromosome anomalies in your baby."

"Amniocentesis?" I echo. "Is it necessary?" I don't ask my real question: *How dangerous is it?*

"The water on the baby's brain could be the result of a chromosome defect," he explains. "In that case

26

there would likely be other serious problems with the baby."

I force myself to say the words. "If there is a chromosome problem, does that mean my baby will die?"

The doctor's tone softens, but his words are clear, distinct. "If there were a *lethal* chromosome combination, there would be no hope. We would implant no shunt, nor would we use any extraordinary measures to save the baby."

I feel weak inside. "What would happen?"

Dr. Anzaldo measures his words carefully. "You would carry the baby, deliver it naturally, and the baby would either die or live out its existence as . . ."

"As a vegetable?"

"Yes."

Now I comprehend why Dr. Anzaldo wanted Bill here today. I sit unmoving, my nerves suddenly raw, stripped of their protective veneer. My body feels limp, buffeted, like a sapling shaken by a storm. How I wish I could reach out this moment for Bill's supportive arms.

This new possibility I find most abhorrent of all— that my baby might be forced to live out its life as a prisoner of its own damaged brain, perhaps cached away for years in an institution. I can draw from the reserves of my mind to think of coping with a retarded child or even suffering through my baby's death.

But not this other thing. That I cannot cope with. I cannot see how such a tragedy could be honoring to God. I don't pretend to understand His ways. I only know He does not make mistakes, even in this. I must remember I can trust Him even when I cannot trace Him.

My Jesus, I'm soul-weary and body-spent. But I'm grateful that today's test showed no further deterioration in the baby. For a few days, at least, a reprieve. I wait on You, Lord, and trust You for tomorrow . . . and my baby's tomorrows.

FRIDAY, DECEMBER 4

I REMEMBER: FOUR YEARS AGO.

A doctor tells me I have cancer. A lump the size of a jawbreaker in my breast. Rock-hard. Dangerous. Deadly. He utters the dreaded word: Mastectomy.

I check into the hospital. Prepare mentally, emotionally for loss. Stare naked in a mirror, knowing I am defenseless. I am shaken, brought starkly, unceremoniously face to chilling face with my own mortality.

Prayer—impassioned, desperate. Prayer through the night till comfort swells around me like encompassing arms.

In the morning: Surgery. The doctor is incredulous. No cancer. Just a thick cyst, benign.

God's miracle.

But now: I am more shaken by the prospect of my unborn baby's death than I was by the threat of my own demise.

Dear God, I struggle with the question: Can I expect another miracle?

SUNDAY, DECEMBER 6

W E ARE IN THE CAR READY to leave for church. But our two-year-old automobile won't start. We sit waiting, trying the engine every few minutes. Finally we give up and stay home.

I feel betrayed. I crave spiritual nourishment. Doesn't God want me in church this morning?

Before the morning is over, our refrigerator malfunctions and the freezer overflows with ice. We spend the day trying to repair it. Nothing helps.

I feel angry, frustrated, exhausted. I want to cry out, *Lord, isn't it enough that I'm already hurting? Must You add insult to injury?*

I glimpse a truth—the terrible toll incidental problems take on a family in the midst of crisis. *Our* family.

These days I am walking a tightrope, attempting to maintain my balance, trying not to give in to the weight and implications of my unborn baby's critical condition. But in walking this tightrope of emotional control, I find myself assailed and nearly blown over by the gathering winds of random troubles.

TUESDAY, DECEMBER 8

Yesterday, another ultrasound. I'm becoming a regular customer.

This morning Dr. Anzaldo telephones and says in his buoyant voice, "I've got only good news! Your little baby showed no further deterioration whatever. In fact, in some of the pictures the baby appeared to have even a little more brain tissue than before."

Oh, God, dare I hope for healing? May I stake my dreams on this baby after all?

Dr. Anzaldo goes on to say that my blood test showed no spina bifida or other spinal deformities in the baby. Of course, this test has nothing to do with the chromosome count, which we will not hear about for another three or four weeks. But I rejoice that the spinal abnormalities have been ruled out.

Lord, You give me hope. Please increase my baby's brain tissue. Cause the deadly fluid to recede.

And help me cope with the problems we face as a family—the unpredictable annoyances that inflict no wounds but rub against the grain like sandpaper, abrasively wearing us down.

MONDAY, DECEMBER 14

Bill goes with me to the hospital this morning. I have the ultrasound at 7:45 A.M., but I'm not able to see the doctor until 11:45. The waiting is an ordeal. I know Bill is nervous about missing so many hours of work—and upset that our car, after all its repairs, is still not working right.

Dr. Anzaldo seems pleased that Bill is here today. He wants to talk to both of us about our baby (a Misty Lynne instead of a Jonathan, according to last Friday's ultrasound!). He tells us there appears to be a slight worsening of the hydrocephalus. He wants me to come back for my next sonogram in three days to determine if the baby is actually deteriorating. If she is, then he will send me to San Francisco for the experimental surgery.

The news devastates me, not only because I dread to think of the baby's condition getting worse, but also because there couldn't be a more inopportune time to go to San Francisco—the week before Christmas!

I confess: I have no Christmas spirit as it is—no energy to shop, bake, or put up a tree. In fact, the shopping has been dutiful and sporadic; there has been no baking and probably won't be; and Kim and David will decorate the tree by themselves. For their sakes, and Heather's, I want to make the most of the Christmas season, but with our lives in such an upheaval and our baby's life hanging in the balance, a Christmas celebration becomes secondary. Even incidental.

I return home from the doctor frustrated by a long day with no good news. I feel fragmented, vulnerable. I'm physically exhausted from the hours of waiting in the hospital, and tonight I'm plagued by those nagging false labor pains that inevitably punctuate the last months of pregnancy.

I don't feel well equipped to handle long-term crises. Just when I summon a measure of optimism and control, something happens to knock me off that balanced line. It staggers me to know my baby is getting worse.

Oh, God, only You can carry me through this.

TUESDAY, DECEMBER 15

I AM IN LABOR—CONTRACTIONS coming harder, faster. My body balks with weariness against this unexpected onslaught.

Bill drives me to the hospital. It's after midnight. Still Monday to me. I've had no sleep. I yearn for my own bed. How can I face the task of labor tonight—the commotion and confusion, doctors probing, nurses hovering, the inevitable, escalating pains, and—oh, God!—premature childbirth!

Can my baby possibly survive this soon?

Two A.M. I'm admitted to the labor and delivery high-risk intensive care unit. A nurse inserts an IV with medication to stop my contractions; another attaches electrodes to my skin and places a wide belt snugly around my abdomen. My mind races. What is this with straps and wires and electrodes? I feel like a guinea pig or an unwilling victim in some Frankenstein experiment.

But no. The wires run from the belt and electrodes to a fetal monitor that delivers a continuous graph like a ticker tape, tracing my contractions and the baby's heartbeat simultaneously.

I lie here feeling terrified, alone. My prayers are like dark, frantic birds caught in a whirlwind, flying blind, scattered in every direction at once. I am powerless, strapped to this hideous bed, staring holes in the ceiling. The contractions persist—a rock-hard belly, muscles stretching like elastic bands, then momentary release and relief.

My baby nudges the flesh-wall between us. A signal, a sign. *I'm still here. With you. In you.*

Child, I know you are. The machine beside me amplifies the sound of you. Your comforting music echoes against these drab hospital walls, speaking life to me. I fall asleep savoring the rhythmic, pulsating "glub-bity-glub" of your heartbeat.

Morning: Dr. Anzaldo arrives, assures me my contractions are stabilized, and apologizes for not warning
me earlier that my condition is susceptible to premature
delivery. I have an "irritated uterus" brought on by excess amniotic fluid. My baby, being brain-damaged,
does not swallow the water properly, and so her normal
circulation of fluids is interrupted, causing an abnormal
amount of water to accumulate in the sac.

*Oh, my poor little one, that even swallowing should
come so difficult for you! Will you drown in your own bitter
fluids?*

I am distracted from my somber musings by a
steady stream of nurses passing through my room,
chatting and friendly. I learn that because I'm a candidate for experimental fetal surgery, the hospital staff
considers me a fascinating case study. One nurse admits, "Your chart sure is popular. I've been trying to get
hold of it all day to read!"

I could almost be amused. If fear hadn't already
numbed me.

WEDNESDAY, DECEMBER 16

MOTHER HAS FLOWN TWO thousand miles to be with
me! Bill drives her straight from the airport to the hospital. My relief is inexpressible. I am shameless. I feel a
physical yearning for my mother's arms. She—if anyone—can make the hurt go away.

My mother and I are bound by emotional ties far
stronger than the umbilical cord that once made us one.
We have never felt the alienation some mothers and
daughters experience. We are fiercely protective of each
other. Neither of us can bear to see the other in pain.

It appears we will be forced by circumstances to
resume our bygone roles of mother and child. The doctor has confined me to bed for the duration of my
pregnancy to minimize the prospect of premature delivery. I won't be able to wait on myself or fix a meal or

care for my children. I am almost grateful to be relieved of these duties. I yearn to become my mother's child again, to accept unabashedly her comfort and solace.

I remember when I was a child I almost liked being sick so I could escape the exacting, uncaring world and stay home from school with my mother. That's what I want to do now—retreat from the burdens and pressures, abdicate adulthood, and be cuddled and coddled again. I want permission to escape the pain. I don't want to face the consequences of creating a child who, one way or another, will demand more of me than I can possibly give. How can I face the ultimate sacrifice of mothering a damaged child, a dying child?

After lunch, Bill and Mother accompany me to radiology for another ultrasound. When the doctor points at the flitting image on the screen and says, "See, the baby's looking right at us," my mother beams, "Oh, what a cute little face!"

How grateful I am for such a spontaneous, grandmotherly reaction in the face of our dismal, unnatural situation. I desperately miss that sense of shared wonder and joy I've known in past pregnancies. This pregnancy brings only shared anxieties. I feel robbed, but it is a robbery I cannot begin to speak of.

Following the ultrasound, we wait in my hospital room until early evening for the results that will determine whether or not I undergo the experimental surgery. There is vague talk among the staff that the hospital helicopter may fly me to the airport for a private flight to San Francisco.

I dread the thought of being shipped off to San Francisco. All I want to do is go home and be with my mother. But my contractions are increasing again as my tension mounts.

When Dr. Anzaldo finally arrives with the ultrasound results, his expression is inscrutable. He says, "It looks like there's been no change in the baby after all."

Hope rises in me like a flag.

"Then what about San Francisco?" Bill asks.

"San Francisco is out. I talked with their doctors this afternoon. We agree that if there's any further deterioration, we'll go ahead and deliver the baby prematurely." Dr. Anzaldo pats my hand encouragingly. "Meanwhile, we'll try to control your contractions with complete bed rest and medication."

"Then may I go home tonight?" I venture.

"If your contractions have stopped."

"They have—or they will—now that I know the baby's not worse and I don't have to go to San Francisco!"

MONDAY, DECEMBER 21

HOME. FIVE DAYS ALREADY.

This isn't working out—I'm supposed to stay calm not get upset—the contractions keep coming—why doesn't the medicine make them stop?—Mother is sick and I have to lie here watching her work, waiting on me, cooking and cleaning, chasing after Heather—I ache for her and me—everyone is on edge—I want to scream!

TUESDAY, DECEMBER 22

GRAPPLING
groping
grasping
grappling with fear
groping through this nightmare
grasping for the faintest gleam of hope. A gift. For Christmas. *God, is that too much to ask?*

Another ultrasound today. The radiologist lets it slip. The baby's hydrocephalus is not a routine type. A tumor is blocking an area in the cerebellum that controls coordination. The child may have cerebral palsy.

I force out the words, "What is the prognosis for my baby?"

Silence. Then: "It doesn't look good."

So there it is. No gift for Christmas. No flimsy thread of hope to seize upon just for the Holidays. Just raw reality—a lump of coal in the stocking. *Virginia, there never was a Santa Claus anyway.*

But God, there's You. I'm grappling with You for a miracle, groping for faith, grasping the raveling threads of hope. Override this bitter disappointment. See me through. God, I'm so aware of my frailties—my fears, my exhaustion, my grief. Hold me in Your arms. Be my joy and peace.

THURSDAY, DECEMBER 24

CHRISTMAS EVE.

My contractions begin early and intensify so that by evening I'm afraid I'll welcome Christmas from a hospital bed. I dread the thought of missing Christmas at home, especially watching the children open their gifts. I want to see Heather's expression on Christmas morning when she discovers her new toys.

Bill, Kim, and David go to his sister Annette's for an old-fashioned Italian lasagna dinner. Mother and I spend the evening lying on my bed timing my contractions.

"Okay, another one," I say as my abdomen hardens.

With her eyes on her watch, Mother murmurs, "Twenty . . . thirty . . . forty seconds. Four minutes apart." So it goes for what seems like hours.

Between contractions we talk and reminisce, wondering how the rest of the family is celebrating Christmas Eve—Daddy, my brother Steve and his wife June in Michigan, my Grandmother Gift alone in Indiana, Aunt Ginny and Uncle Alan in Australia . . .

"One thing we can be sure of," quips Mother. "None of them are doing what *we're* doing."

Around 8 P.M., Daddy telephones from Michigan. He's alone, concerned about us. His deep, familiar voice soothes me. My contractions begin to abate.

Mother and I talk confidentially about the Lord— about how faithful He has been to us over the years and about His purpose in giving us the problems we face. I treasure these moments, this closeness with Mother, the connection we both feel with God. In my heart, it is as much Christmas as it ever has been or ever could be.

FRIDAY, DECEMBER 25

CHRISTMAS DAY. SURPRISINGLY pleasant considering the shadow of sadness darkening our days. My sister Susi and her husband Dan come this afternoon bearing gifts, along with ham, turkey, and all the trimmings for a scrumptious dinner.

We stuff ourselves unashamedly, open presents, chat about everything and nothing, play Yahtzee, and devour bowls of hot, buttered popcorn. From my bed on the couch I savor every moment. I'm reminded of Susi's and my growing-up years when on cold winter evenings we popped corn, played Monopoly or Rook, and thrived on being together.

TUESDAY, DECEMBER 29

I'VE BEEN THROUGH A STRUGGLE these past weeks trying to determine how best to pray regarding our baby and her predicament. I've reached three separate conclusions.

First, as a child of God and a joint-heir with Christ, I have access to the powers of the universe and the right to petition God with my requests. I have the right and the invitation from God Himself to express my desires, to entreat Him on my behalf. I have done this. I have prayed for a miracle for my baby, a miracle of complete healing.

At the same time, I have become convinced of the necessity of committing this child and her future completely to God, of turning her over to Him anew each time I feel the impulse to hold tight with my own will and wishes. She belongs to Jesus first of all.

Jesus, she is Yours and if You choose to give her to me for any length of time or no time at all, it is Your choice, Your will, and therefore mine too. She is in the blessed palm of Your hand just as I am.

The third thing that has been impressed upon my heart these past days is to thank God for this child—just as she is, whatever her condition, whatever her future. I thank God for her because I know He will use her life to honor Himself and to bless others, whether her life lasts for moments, days, or years. I believe He will bring good from the experiences we consider tragedies; He will make perfect the imperfect; He will bring joy from mourning.

WEDNESDAY, DECEMBER 30

DR. ANZALDO TELEPHONES AFTER DINNER. "I received the results back on the chromosome test," he says. "I'd like you and Bill to come into my office tomorrow morning to discuss them."

"Can't you tell us the results now, over the phone?" I urge.

"I'd rather we talk in person."

"Won't you please give us some idea now?" I persist. "I can't bear to go another night without knowing."

Bill, on the extension, says quietly, "Carole, I think he's trying to tell us it's bad news."

"Is that it? Is it the fatal chromosome combination you mentioned before?"

Dr. Anzaldo clears his throat uncomfortably. "I really don't like giving patients news like this over the phone, but it looks like you're forcing me into it."

"Yes, I am," I say firmly. "I want to know."

He tells us as gently as he can what I prayed I would never hear. "Your baby has multiple problems that are inconsistent with life."

"You mean the lethal chromosome combination," I acknowledge. Already everything inside me is quietly shattering.

"Yes," he replies reluctantly. "She has three chromosomes on #18. Babies with this particular combination have no chance of survival." He goes on to say that our little girl may live for hours, days, weeks, or as long as six months. But there are so many things wrong with her that she has no chance for a full-term life. She will be virtually a vegetable for however long she lives.

So there it is—the inconceivable, the impossible, the unthinkable.

As I continue listening to the doctor's words, numbness takes over. I am almost grateful for the sensation. I don't want to feel anything. I want to go on, participate in what's going on around me, continue my normal routine without letting this news devastate me. I don't want to collapse in grief or fall apart emotionally. I don't want this to make a difference.

It will. I know that. I know the doctor's words can penetrate only so deep, can make me feel the truth to only a limited extent at this time. The reality is that I am still carrying this baby; she still moves and kicks actively, tucked safely beneath my breast. I cannot believe this little unseen daughter carries a death sentence. How can a test I've never seen, a piece of paper or a doctor's words over the phone pronounce death when I still cradle life inside my body? How can death have any meaning for me when my baby still hiccups and squirms and jabs my ribs happily, unsuspectingly? She's still alive. How can she die?

Dr. Anzaldo is still speaking. "I'm taking you off the medication controlling your contractions and I've canceled plans for a C-section. I want you to continue carrying the baby until she comes naturally in a regular vaginal delivery."

I argue with him. "If the baby is going to die anyway, I'd rather have an immediate C-section. How can I go on like this for maybe another two months?"

He replies with equal conviction. "It will be safer for you if you don't have to go through major surgery and two or three months of recovery."

Aloud I accept his decision, but silently, vehemently I protest. I find myself in the untenable position of having to continue carrying a child I know I can never have. Childbirth has always been such a special event for me, a time for giving life, a joyous, unparalleled experience. Now it will mean only death, the beginning of sorrow and loss.

Recently a neighbor's daughter learned that her unborn child had died inside her. She had to carry the child another week and give birth to a dead baby. At the time I thought, That is one experience in life I could not handle, the thing I fear most of all. Now, bitter irony! I must carry a live baby, knowing she will die shortly after birth.

After Dr. Anzaldo's call, we are all strangely silent, controlled. No tears, no railing, no laments. I do not scream; the earth does not quake; my heart does not stop. There is no thunderclap, only paralysis and a slow, creeping chill invading my veins, barely perceptible. My reality is still these vital baby thrusts within.

Bill telephones our friends and relatives to tell them of our baby's fatal condition. I hear his voice break as he repeats the news.

Mother and I go to Heather's room and sit with her on the bed. Heather playfully throws her head back, hits the wall, and immediately begins to wail. I gather her into my arms and hold her, whispering endearments. As I do so, I am struck by the realization that I will never be able to hold and comfort my unborn daughter to ease away her troubles.

I begin to weep with Heather, burying my face against her fine blonde hair. When she sees me crying, she cries all the harder, obviously puzzled and dismayed that I have joined her in her tears. As we weep, Mother puts her arms around us both and holds us close.

SATURDAY, JANUARY 2

WHEN MY BABY KICKS OR SQUIRMS, my impulse still is to say, "Bill . . . Mother! Come feel the baby move!"

I stop myself. Who wants to take pleasure in the antics of a baby who is going to die?

Incredibly, I still want to enjoy her, marvel over her, be proud of her existence. I feel almost ashamed of these feelings, as if I have lost the right to be a proud mother. I resent the fact that my baby has become an unspeakable subject. I sense I would be considered a curious oddity for taking delight in her now.

So already, before the fact, she is dead to us.

SUNDAY, JANUARY 3

DEATH. THE SPECTER OF DEATH hovers over me, waiting. Not for me, for my baby. We play this waiting game, this bizarre deadly game. Waiting.

I've seen Death's face before. No stranger is he. He's waited for me in the past.

When I was three, a mosquito bite sent me spinning into the convulsions and coma of sleeping sickness. Encephalitis—an insidious inflammation of the brain. The doctors told my parents I would probably die. "It's better that way," they said. "If she lived, she'd likely be a vegetable."

My mother promised God my life if He would heal me.

He did.

When I was seven, I went into shock following a tonsillectomy. My heart stopped beating. I turned blue. Death thought he had me. But a watchful nurse sprang into action and brought me back.

Round three: The breast cancer diagnosis four years ago. I sparred with Death again—and won.

But today: Death waits for my baby.

I wonder. Will someone snatch my tiny daughter from Death's grip, keep her from being a vegetable, start her heart beating again when life is gone?

Or is Death grinning gleefully, knowing he has won this round?

MONDAY, JANUARY 4

Raining today.
Still waiting.
Rain-gloom. Inside and out.
Still, still waiting.

Absurd as it is, we all go about our business as if life were normal. The holidays are over (were there actually holidays?). Bill goes back to work, Kim and David back to school. Mother fixes ham and scalloped potatoes. We watch old movies on TV.

One bright spot: Roland Seboldt, book editor at Augsburg, telephones from Minneapolis. He's heard about the baby. He shares my grief. He speaks from heart-wrenching experience. Recently his grown son died. I am in awe of Roland. I can't imagine losing a child after a love-investment of so many years. I think of how profoundly I feel about a baby I've loved only months and never seen. How must it be for Roland?

Can grief be measured? Is it easier to lose an infant than an adult child? Reasonably, it seems so. Then again, a child is a child is a child. Does a child, even when he grows old and gray, ever stop being your child? Or is a damaged, unfinished infant any less your child?

Over the phone, across the miles, Roland and I weep for each other, not openly, but the tears are in our voices. And when I hang up, I feel pleasantly buoyed by Roland's sturdy faith and compassion.

I am blessed. I don't even mind that it's raining.

TUESDAY, JANUARY 5

I AM HAVING CONSTANT contractions and unrelieved discomfort from the excess buildup of amniotic fluid. My abdomen is so distended, it is difficult to breathe. Even Dr. Anzaldo admits I couldn't possibly get much larger. Severe heartburn prevents me from eating much now. Still, I've gained seven pounds just this past week, all of it amniotic fluid. I look at least ten months pregnant, or as if I were carrying a great, ripe watermelon under my clothes.

WEDNESDAY, JANUARY 6

MY CONTRACTIONS ARE BECOMING more painful, and I have noticed a slight "bloody show." Mother keeps insisting I go to the hospital. As my discomfort increases, so does her nervousness. My friend Sheila Cragg, who is visiting us today, urges me to go too.

"I don't know how to deliver a baby, do you, Sheila?" my mother remarks more than once. She isn't trying to be funny; she means it.

"Not me!" Sheila exclaims, and decides it's time for her to be going.

Reluctantly I telephone Bill at work and tell him I'd better get to the hospital.

"Can you wait an hour—until I'm through with work?" he wants to know.

"I'm not sure," I reply between contractions.

"Okay, I'll be right there."

At the hospital, the staff monitors my contractions

for two hours. The general consensus is that the baby won't be born tonight. Apparently my cervix isn't at all effaced or dilated. I'm disappointed by the false alarm.

Dr. Anzaldo, who isn't on call tonight, pays us an unexpected visit. When he enters the room we see his feet moving beneath the curtain as he performs his little tap dance of greeting. Then he whisks the curtain aside and warms us with his broad, boyish grin. He strides over and takes my hand, gently kissing my cheek as if we were comfortable, longtime friends.

We exchange the usual pleasantries. Then he sits down, assumes a casual pose, and begins a confidential discussion about what we can expect when the baby is born. He wants to know how we feel about things and whether we understand the situation clearly.

"The baby may come in the next couple of days," he says. "Because there is so much fluid buildup, you are having strong contractions, but the baby, being seven weeks premature, is still small, around four pounds. She hasn't settled into the birth position where her head would push on the cervix as in normal births. She is still basically free-floating, which means you may have a long, hard labor."

He again explains that the baby will probably be born alive and may even seem to do all right for the first few hours. But within a week she will likely succumb to her many physical problems—although she could possibly live as long as six months.

Dr. Anzaldo assures us that the staff is aware of the situation. Everyone understands that no heroic or extraordinary measures will be taken to keep the baby alive—no respirator, no IVs, no surgeries. His expression softens as he adds, "She will be fed and kept warm, that is all."

"May we spend time with her and hold her?" I ask.

"Of course," he replies with feeling. "Some parents refuse to become emotionally involved with such a child. They don't even want to see their baby, while others want to give the child as much love and attention as they can while the infant lives. It's up to you."

My voice catches as I reply, "Bill and I—we both feel strongly about this. We want to be with our baby and love her as much as possible . . . for however long we have her."

Even as Dr. Anzaldo continues talking to us about what we will face in the days ahead, a single refrain runs through my mind, again and again: *This baby is for Jesus . . . this baby is for Jesus.*

Our tiny Misty Lynne Page, our little momentary child, will be a whole, complete person just as I asked, but in God's chosen way.

Oh, Lord, when the times comes, please give me the grace to release her to You without bitterness or despair.

THURSDAY, JANUARY 7

Hard, unrelenting contractions. But after last night's false alarm I'm not about to go to the hospital until I'm sure it's the real thing.

Mother grows increasingly concerned, suffering through each pain with me, monitoring my contractions. By the time Bill arrives home from work I'm considering going to the hospital. But he doesn't seem especially concerned; he's more intent on finding out about his dinner. So I decide to wait it out a while longer.

Liz Wilderman, a friend from church, brings us dinner at 6 P.M. She asks to see me, but I feel too bad to see anyone. Mother brings me in a plate of food. I sit up in bed and try to eat a bite or two, then lie back down. My contractions are coming only a minute apart, so forceful I can barely move. I want to stay right here in bed, but I realize I'd better get to the hospital.

Once Mother realizes I'm serious about going to the hospital, she convinces Bill to call Labor and Delivery to tell them I'm coming in. By now the crescendos of pain have immobilized me, so both Mother and Bill have to help me dress. I don't bother with makeup or combing my hair (a rarity for me to skip such "necessities"). I waddle to the car, clamber awkwardly into the front seat, and Bill and I are off, facing the night traffic on the freeway.

"I'm driving a little over the speed limit," Bill informs me (a nearly unthinkable deed for him).

"Good!" I say emphatically. I'm growing more and more concerned. My contractions are now frighteningly reminiscent of what I felt just before the bearing-down pains with Heather. It can't be! The bag of waters hasn't begun to leak as it did early in labor with my three previous pregnancies.

As we pull up to the Memorial Hospital Medical Center in Long Beach, I tell Bill, "Take me directly up to the maternity floor, then go park the car. I can't walk alone or wait for you in the lobby." Privately I'm not sure I can make the long walk even *with* Bill's help.

As we enter the hospital lobby, I feel a slight leaking sensation. Grimly we face the usual interminable wait at the elevators. I lean against Bill and wonder if I will collapse right here on the spot. Finally an elevator arrives. The doors roll open, seemingly in slow motion. The elevator is jammed with people standing their ground, staring blankly at me. I groan inwardly. We squeeze in anyway, prompting a few startled glances and raised eyebrows. Silently I utter, *Thank God we're almost there!*

We get off at the second floor and walk the dozen or more steps to the big double doors marked "Labor and Delivery Suite." Just as we pass through the doors, I feel a sudden, horrifying gush of water. I look down. My slacks are drenched. Water continues to pour all over the linoleum floor. Desperately I cry, "Help! My water broke!"

Several nurses behind the desk look up in puzzlement, then spring into action. They lead me briskly down the hall to a labor room while the amniotic fluid continues to gush. Our feet are slipping and sliding. We can scarcely walk on the slick, wet tile. Fighting my own panic, I try to explain to the baffled nurses the reason for the flood. As soon as I mention hydrocephalus, they understand.

In the labor room, while the torrent continues, the nurses attempt to help me undress. I'm stunned by the deluge. No one had warned me it would be like this. Even when Bill and Mother and I had joked about the possible "flood," I had never imagined facing such a helpless, terrifying situation as this.

Even more frightening, I'm beginning to have bearing-down pains. Dr. Elizabeth Irwin, the doctor on call, starts to check me. "The baby's coming now," I tell her urgently. "I have to push."

She nods agreement. "The baby's right there," she tells the nurses. "Let's get her to the delivery room, stat!"

They wheel me, bed and all, at what seems break-neck speed, down the hall to the delivery suite. All the while a nurse keeps instructing me, "Don't push, just pant!" I've never panted so hard in my life.

In the delivery room, everyone moves rapidly, shouting orders, wheeling equipment into place. One nurse's voice booms above the others. "Tell Dr. Evans to scrub!"

In moments the attendants lift me onto the delivery table, drape my trembling legs, and place my feet in the stirrups. With every explosive contraction I'm sure the baby will come.

"No time for Dr. Evans!" Dr. Irwin declares. She tells me, "Pant through one more contraction and we'll be ready." After two more contractions she makes the incision for the episiotomy. "Now you can push."

I hardly push at all and the baby's head emerges.

Dr. Irwin suctions her, then tells me to push again on the next contraction. The baby slips out easily. "Do you want to see the baby?" she asks tentatively.

"Yes," I say softly. "I want to spend as much time as possible with her."

A nurse brings her over, wrapped loosely in a little blanket, and lays her on my chest. I lift my head slightly and look at her.

In one startling glance I see that my baby is not normal. She is small (three pounds, seventeen inches long, I learn later), and her coloring is slightly purplish. Most noticeable are her irregular features—a head a little larger than normal, ears tucked back against her head. She looks like a Down's syndrome child with slanted, nearly closed eyes and a flat nose with no bridge. But she also has an appealing rosebud mouth and striking black curly hair. I cradle her and whisper, "Poor little thing."

Her breathing is irregular; the sides of her chest cave in with every gasp. There is a strange little triangular indentation in the center of her chest and only the slightest trace of pale pink nipples. Her legs and arms are long. Her arms are crossed on her chest, her legs drawn up against her body. Her fingers and toes are long and white, her nails tiny and red, her left thumb partially deformed. She makes a few little sounds, tiny bleats, as if trying to cry. But she can't quite manage it.

I gaze at her, my feelings mixed. I'm shocked by her poor appearance. I never expected her to look so obviously unnatural, unsalvageable. I'm struck by the certainty that there is no way she can or should survive; there is no hope for any sort of meaningful life.

I feel a surprisingly calm acceptance of that fact. And in a way I feel relief—relief that my baby, whose entire genetic nature has already sentenced her to death, is not a beautiful, rosy-cheeked, normal-looking baby. Such a deceptive appearance would make our inevitable parting even more unbearable.

I also feel a sense of loving acceptance of Misty just as she is. I love her, and she is mine to cradle and cuddle for however long she lives. I talk softly to her

47

and kiss the tiny dark curls on the top of her head and tell her Jesus loves her.

After a few minutes a nurse comes and takes Misty Lynne over to a little table while the attendants prepare to take me to the recovery room.

Bill arrives at last in a scrub gown, gives me a brief, reassuring kiss, and goes to see Misty. In all the confusion I hardly realized he wasn't here for the delivery! He had gone down to move the car and by the time he returned, the delivery was over. When we compare notes, we learn I arrived at the hospital at 6:30 P.M. Misty was born at 6:38!

"She would have been born four minutes earlier if I hadn't done a good job of panting instead of pushing," I tell Bill. Neither of us can believe what a close call it was. How close I came to delivering the baby at home—or in the car on the freeway! I will forever shudder at the chance we took without even realizing it.

Bill, too, is shocked by Misty's appearance. Dr. Anzaldo never mentioned that the baby could have the Mongoloid characteristics, although he had said there could be facial deformities. His remark had baffled me, but with so many other concerns, I dismissed his words from my mind. Bill, too—his eyes red-rimmed, his gaze tender—sees that there is no hope of any kind for our little daughter in this life. But, clearly, he too loves her.

We ask the nurses how long they think she will live. After a little persistence on our part, they finally admit they doubt she will live through the night. All of us are aware that there will be no heroic measures on her behalf. She will live only as long as her little lungs can support her with air.

A nurse tells me I can have the baby with me as long as I wish after I spend an hour in the recovery room. I'm reluctant for us to be separated even for an hour, but I don't protest. So while an orderly wheels me to recovery, Misty is taken to another room and Bill goes to make phone calls to our family.

For the first time I have a chance to relax and allow my mind to reflect on all that has happened during the past hour. I can't get over how quickly everything has occurred. After so many weeks of growing discomfort from the abnormal buildup of fluid, after the countless days of anxiety, of rising hopes and dashed hopes, after days of painful, seemingly unproductive contractions—now it is all behind me. The delivery is over. I no longer have to wonder how our baby will look or how I will feel and react.

Perhaps what surprises me most of all is the peace and acceptance I feel. I sense the Lord's presence, His control over all that is happening. I feel no anguish, no terrible sense of desolation, no desire to blame God or myself or anyone else. I sense a purpose to my circumstances. A Scripture verse plays over and over in my mind: "Thou wilt keep him in perfect peace whose mind is stayed on thee, because he trusteth in thee." As I lie here savoring those words, even the trembling in my legs begins to subside.

After a while a telephone rings. I hear the nurse mention my name. Then she comes and tells me they are bringing the baby to me here in the recovery room. I suspect it's because Misty isn't doing well. The orderlies move my bed to a private section of the room and draw the curtain. Bill enters, his eyes glistening with unshed tears. A young blonde nurse follows with our baby.

I take Misty in my arms. Her complexion is more purplish than before. She isn't moving as much, and her breathing is more irregular.

"I was holding her and taking her picture in the other room," Bill tells me. He snaps a couple of shots of me holding her. Then we both talk to her and kiss her. We assure her that Mommy and Daddy love her and Jesus loves her too, and that soon she will be with Jesus and He will make her a complete person—beautiful and healthy and whole.

I rub her cheek and little chin. Whenever I touch

her chin, her tiny oval mouth makes an arc, sweetly reminiscent of a smile. Still, her eyes never quite open or focus; there is nothing to indicate that she is aware of us. But we love her and tell her so.

Within the hour my mother, Kim, and David arrive at the hospital with Bill's sister Annette. The nurses bend the rules and allow my mother to come in and be with me and the baby for a few minutes.

Mother comes to me with open arms. She holds me and weeps. Somehow I still feel no need to cry. She sits beside me, and we spend a few minutes talking and examining Misty.

Mother, too, is shocked by Misty's appearance. Bill hadn't warned her what to expect. She also realizes that Misty will find a meaningful life only in heaven.

Then, as I touch Misty's face, I know she is gone. I kiss my little daughter one last time and hand her gently back to the nurse.

"Your husband wants to show the baby to your other children," she says. "I'm not sure that's a good idea. It could be quite traumatic for them."

We debate the question a minute or two. Finally I tell her, "If they really want to see Misty, they should."

When Bill returns to my room a little later, he tells me what happened when he showed Kim and David their little sister. "A nurse led us to a private office," he says. "Then she brought Misty in wrapped in her little blanket and gave her to me. I let Kim and David see her. They cried. We all cried. Then we gathered in a circle and prayed and thanked God for Misty and for the brief time we had her. When I looked over at the nurses, they were watching with tears in their eyes."

He squeezes my hand and adds, "Before I left, one of the nurses told me they had never seen a family react so well in such devastating circumstances. She said many parents refuse to have anything to do with their babies when they know they are going to lose them or when the child has such serious problems." He smiles wanly. "We were a testimony to those nurses, Carole. We can be thankful for that."

Evening: Bill, Mother, and the children go home. I'm in my assigned room for the night, alone for the first time today. I'm too keyed up to sleep. I am on a spiritual and emotional plane that defies reason. I have just gone through a traumatic birth followed by the death of my child, and yet, incredibly, I feel all right, at peace, held together by the Lord's boundless grace.

I marvel that I still feel no real grief, no overwhelming sorrow. I feel a sense of strength, a knowledge of having just come through one of the most difficult and important moments of my life, and Jesus has been with me every moment.

It is an awesome sensation, this almost physical, tangible awareness of God's presence. His arms cradling me even as I lie here. His whispering comfort in my heart, more precious than a mother's soothing words. How can I think of loss and death when I am so filled with Him this moment, when all my needs are met in His ministering Spirit, when His love surrounds and satisfies me like a warm, protective womb?

FRIDAY, JANUARY 8

MORNING. WAKEFULNESS COMES over me in slivers of consciousness like the first glints of sunlight beaming through my hospital window. Even in my groggy state of semi-awareness, I am swathed in peace, buoyed by a sense of well-being. Jesus held me through the night!

One by one my memory fills in the momentary blanks of yesterday's traumatic events—Misty's birth, Misty's death. The peace remains, larger than reality itself.

Strange, I muse silently. This is the first time I've had a sound night's sleep after the birth of one of my children. Always before I tossed and turned, worried about my newborn baby, fearful of unforeseen complications. But Misty is beyond all that, immune to accident or illness, safe in the arms of Jesus. I don't have to worry about her ever again.

Then, just as I am beginning to think this grief business is going to be a snap, my sense of well-being is jarred by a small commotion on the other side of my curtain. Nurses are helping someone into the empty bed beside me. I hear a woman's muffled sobbing and soft voices trying to calm and comfort. From the nurses' remarks, I realize the young woman beside me has also just lost her baby.

Her crying bothers me. It eats at the edges of my peace. I feel sorry for this broken, unseen woman. I ache for her. Then it strikes me. I share her loss. I am the same as she—a mother who has just lost her child. Yet I'm not crying. I don't even feel like crying. *Is something wrong with me?*

Shortly, the day begins in earnest. Nurses bustle about, and breakfast trays clatter. My new roommate, Esther, and I greet each other, tentatively at first but warming quickly, two strangers with the deepest of common bonds. Gradually we share our separate losses with each other. She tells me she lost a son, five months along, because of an incompetent cervix. In sharing, we each find a small measure of comfort.

We are both relieved that we have been placed in a section of the hospital where there are no babies, no nursing mothers, no infant cries, no rooming in. We are glad to be roommates, free to express our sadness or disappointment without dampening the spirits of some new mother.

Only occasionally during the day do I feel a real pang of disappointment or a shard of grief. When a woman from the Records Department comes to take down information for Misty's birth certificate, I am about to ask her if she also wants information for the death certificate. But as she blithely hands me a sheet of information about obtaining copies of birth certificates for future school records, I realize with a start that she has no idea that Misty died.

Then, just outside the shower room, I meet my former hospital roommate from three weeks ago. She's due to have her baby by C-section this coming week. She flinches noticeably when I tell her my baby died. I immediately regret having told her. I feel unnerved, as if I've unwittingly violated some unspoken code. Returning to my room, it occurs to me that death is a *verboten* subject among the living.

I cry only once today, just after Pastor Gene Wood's visit to discuss what he will say at Misty's funeral. The reality of having to face an actual funeral hits me for the first time. I want to put this whole devastating experience with Misty behind me. A funeral represents another emotional hurdle to face. Won't it only prolong the pain? My feelings surge between opposing poles: *I don't want a funeral at all. But, of course, Misty must have a funeral!*

Early in the evening Dr. Anzaldo dismisses me. "You're doing fine," he says. "There's no reason to stay any longer."

Before Bill and I leave the hospital, Dr. Anzaldo stops by my room again just to talk. He sits down with the casual air of a comfortable old friend. "I want you to know I've grown personally through knowing you," he says seriously. "You might find it surprising, but I've learned from both of you. I'm impressed by the way you two have handled this whole situation. You're really a 'together' couple."

His voice fills unexpectedly with emotion. "In fact, after walking with you through your loss, I appreciate my own children more. I went home the other night and gave my little son and baby daughter an extra hug."

For a moment we lapse into silence, sharing a rare, wordless bond. Then, my own emotions close to the surface, I reply, "We've really appreciated your support, Dr. Anzaldo. Your warmth and concern made things more bearable for us."

He looks pleased. "Well, I never would have told you the bad news about your little baby over the telephone that night if the three of us hadn't already established such a good rapport. Any other couple would have had to come into my office so I could counsel them face to face."

"It's our faith in Christ that has helped us," Bill admits frankly. "We haven't walked alone."

"I know you haven't," Dr. Anzaldo says with what seems a wistful smile.

Minutes later, as Bill begins our drive home, I look at the dashboard clock. It is 6:30 P.M., exactly twenty-four hours since we drove with such haste to the hospital. A single day, and yet what a galaxy of events has passed through those hours! Now it is January 8th and—I realize suddenly—our son David's twelfth birthday!

As I settle in again at home, I feel a profound sense of gratitude to be back in the heart of my family. I am still marveling that I've managed to get through this ordeal with a minimum of anguish. Somehow I've survived, and now I feel only a pleasant sort of numbness. Amazingly, grief hasn't overwhelmed me!

SATURDAY, JANUARY 9

THE EMOTIONAL NOVOCAINE IS wearing off. The first searing pain comes when I open the birth announcement of some friends, boasting of their healthy new son.

I start to cry. I don't want to cry. Since Misty's death I've wept only once briefly in the hospital after Pastor Wood's visit. Now I find myself feeling weepy all day. The least little thing prompts the tears to flow again. Bill is busy making funeral arrangements. He

made most of them on Friday while I was still hospital-
ized, and now he is completing the plans.

Inside, I rebel. I don't want to think about a funeral. I don't want to go to one, especially not to something
elaborate, which it seems apparent Bill is planning.

Finally, in tears I declare, "She was so little and
hardly even here with us. All I want is a short graveside
service, not a big formal service in the chapel with an
organ playing!"

Bill obligingly modifies the arrangements. Misty
will have just a brief, informal graveside service.

Later: Susi and Dan arrive, have dinner with us.
Sheila's home-baked chicken.

That evening Susi, Mother, and I sit together on the
twin bed in Heather's room. Heather slumbers in her
crib while we talk in quiet, confidential tones. Woman-
talk. Mother-daughter sounds. No one can touch us; no
one can comprehend the bond we share. Surely not our
husbands. They move about in another part of the
house. They leave us alone. They know enough not to
intrude. These are sacred moments; our connections run
deep; ties formed in the womb seem to strengthen with
the years.

We talk about Misty, about her dying. I feel my
mother's grief, my sister's grief as vividly as I feel my
own. We are one in mourning. Suddenly Susi begins to
weep, venting her tears in great shuddering sobs. I am
amazed, stunned. In all our years I've never seen her
cry like this. We embrace, weeping together, rocking in
each other's arms. "I love you, Carole," she says. "You
don't know how I've hurt for you these past few weeks.
I've ached so badly, and there wasn't a thing I could do
for you."

I am speechless. Touched beyond words. This is
the little sister of my youth—the tomboy in a Hopalong
Cassidy hat, the mischievous imp who hid when I
called, the ragamuffin in hand-me-down clothes. I never knew her then, although we shared a cramped room

in our parents' little house. Forced to watch her while our parents worked, I alternately resented and ignored her. She played baseball with the boys, skinned her knees, and got black eyes. We were nothing alike. I was studious, awkward, painfully shy. Susi, invariably the performer, witty and gregarious, captivated crowds from the tender age of five.

Perhaps it was the age difference. Or the difference in our personalities. Or the fact that I went away to college just as she entered junior high. We didn't become friends until we were both adults, forging our own lives, homes, and careers.

Now I treasure her companionship. I adore her, stand in awe of her. Sister of my heart.

Tonight most of all. In my grief she has given me a priceless gift: her tears.

SUNDAY, JANUARY 10

I'M DREADING MISTY'S FUNERAL on Tuesday. The thought of seeing her casket and the grave site and of trying to sit through a memorial service leaves me feeling devastated. I remain constantly on the verge of tears.

What's happening to me? I held up through so many weeks of anxiety and uncertainty, of discomfort and pain; and yet now, when seemingly the worst is over, I'm falling apart.

The breaking point comes when Bill casually mentions that there will be twenty-five people coming to our house for dinner after the funeral. He hastily adds, "Don't worry, hon. Our Sunday school class is bringing in the food."

Regardless, I feel suddenly overwhelmed. I look around at the cluttered house and exclaim, "Then you're going to have to clean the house for me!"

He shrugs and says, "People will understand. No one's going to pay attention to how the house looks."

"I'll pay attention," I insist. "It has to be right."

56

"Well, how about your mother? Can't she clean it?"

"You know how ill she's been," I remind him. "Besides, she's all worn out. She's going to Susi's to rest up until the funeral."

"I didn't know."

"Will you clean the house or not?" I persist. "Your employer gave you a week off to get things done."

"I know, but I've got other things to do."

"Well, I can't do it!" I shout. I know I sound shrewish, but I can't help myself. "I'm still recovering from childbirth, plus all the weeks I was laid up."

Bill shows no sign of relenting. It's obvious to me that, in his mind, there is no situation that warrants involving him in housework.

In that instant something in me erupts. I jump up, and for the first time in our marriage I strike Bill soundly on the back and shriek, "Never again in my life will I ever ask you to do anything for me!" I run to the bedroom and slam the door. Slam it so hard, in fact, that when I try to open it, it sticks. I realize with mounting frustration that Bill will have to come and force it open before I can get out.

But at the moment I'm too angry to call for help. In fact, I don't care if I ever get out. I fling myself on the bed and break into great, gulping sobs. I can't stop crying. I feel betrayed by Bill and overcome by hopelessness. Not only have I lost my baby; now my marriage is shattering as well.

I brood, gathering grievances in my mind. In the past few weeks Bill has been so involved with other things—finishing the construction of David's new room, working on this project or that—that he has had little time, sympathy, or compassion for what I've been going through. I was the one having to suffer through this excruciating pregnancy—being confined to bed, enduring heartburn and the awful cramps from being so unnaturally bloated, being forced to restrict all my usual activities—all ultimately for a baby I could never have. The mental anguish was as great as the physical trauma.

All the while Bill went his way, carrying on his usual activities, with only an occasional glance my way and a casual, "How are you feeling, hon?" And from the day my mother appeared, he made himself even more scarce, apparently assuming that with her to wait on me I needed no special attention from him.

Today was the proverbial straw that broke the camel's back. When I struck Bill just now, I felt that no matter how hard I hammered against him, I would never be able to summon even a modicum of sympathy.

After my tears are spent and my grievances counted, I shout through the bedroom door for someone to free me. Bill comes and heaves his weight against the door several times before it pops open.

But the tension between us remains. We argue heatedly in front of Mother and my sister Susi. I'm sure they must think our marriage is on its last legs. The whole incident leaves me more shaken than ever. My spirits sink to a new low. I am carrying not only my burden of grief over Misty, but I also mourn a fifteen-year marriage that has managed to crumble in a single day. I spend the rest of the afternoon in a surfeit of self-pity and tears.

As planned, Mother goes home with Susi in the evening, so I feel lonelier than ever. In a way, I'm glad she has gone. She was exhausted and desperately needed to get away from our situation here. She was nearly as upset as I.

I go to bed totally demoralized. All my spiritual strength has waned; my sense of calm and control has completely evaporated; and I feel on the verge of nervous collapse—all in two short days, for no apparent reason.

As I lie in bed reflecting over the day's events, two important insights gradually take shape in my mind. First, I've discovered that in a time of loss and grief, it takes a while for your emotions to catch up with your head knowledge. What's more, you can't escape feeling the pain. It will catch up with you sooner or later, and I'm beginning to realize . . . the pain is necessary for healing.

The other thing I've learned today is that during a family crisis, the tiny cracks and fissures that every marriage has will likely rupture into monumental proportions—for a time at least. The little things that bother you but that you endure without hardship during normal times become terrible sore spots during a crisis. For a while today I really felt Bill and I no longer had a salvageable marriage. I wondered how I ever could have put up with his unsympathetic nature for fifteen years. I even thought fleetingly that I would like to run away from him, from everything. But those thoughts and feelings, so volatile this afternoon, have faded to mere memory tonight.

At last I fall into an exhausted sleep. But during the night I am awakened by a sudden attack of chills and nausea. I begin to tremble uncontrollably. The sensation strikes panic in me. Desperately I turn to Bill for the warmth and closeness of his arms. For several minutes I sob while he holds me close. I tell him I'm sorry for being angry with him earlier. I glimpse an insight, half-formed: Perhaps tackling projects is Bill's way of handling his grief. He, in turn, apologizes for being so insensitive to my needs. We cling to each other as we never have before. Finally I fall asleep nestled against his chest.

MONDAY, JANUARY 11

I AWAKE FEELING DIZZY and bone-weary. I'm still dreading Misty's funeral tomorrow, but at least I'm not weepy today. I spend most of the morning lying on the couch while Bill cleans house for our company tomorrow.

Without a word he tackles the chores and does an admirable job.

While he works, I decide to relax in the tub. Unexpectedly Bill enters and puts Heather in the bathtub with me. "Oh, Bill, no," I protest. "I'm not up to handling a wiggly, splashing toddler."

From the doorway he replies, "You know she's too hard for anyone else to handle at bath time. Besides," he adds with a twinkle, "I've got to go run the sweeper."

Amazingly, Heather sits still and lets me wash her hair and body. In that commonplace ritual, with her wet, naked baby's body next to mine, all sweet-smelling silk and softness, I feel a surprising, life-affirming joy, akin to the birth experience itself.

Somehow this brief, shared bath helps to lift the aura of death that remains from my birth experience with Misty. I remember afresh Heather's natural birth when the doctor placed her plump, pink body on mine. She opened her eyes with an amazing alertness and nursed eagerly—a separate, unique individual, one with me, the umbilical cord still attached. Those tender memories of her birth are all the more precious to me now.

TUESDAY, JANUARY 12

T HE FUNERAL.

Oh, Father, there is no painless way to lose a child. But You know that. You gave Your Son.

Strange. We don't stop to think that You were a grieving parent too.

The funeral.

Getting ready. Hectic. Everyone tense. David dawdles. Bill scolds. *Hurry up. Get dressed. We're running late!*

Twelve-year-old David, usually so mellow, bristles, snaps back.

I see it coming. A confrontation.

Lord, please, not this morning, of all mornings!

Bill tells David, "How can you act this way? Don't you know your mother's upset?"

We are silenced by David's reply: "Don't *I* have a right to be upset? She was *my* sister too, you know!"

I stare at my son, my only son, no longer a child, not quite a man. His eyes are a mirror of my own grief. And I am reminded that I do not mourn alone today.

We drive through traffic-clogged streets to the cemetery, a strange, silent pilgrimage. Dressed in our Sunday clothes. We could be driving to church, to the mall, anywhere. But no. This is a unique journey—to our daughter's funeral.

My palms are sweaty, my wrists tingle. I dread this day as much as I have ever dreaded anything. I wince at the thought of seeing Misty's casket. It's been five days since I laid her in the nurse's arms. I haven't seen or touched her since then. With a closed casket, I won't see her now. I want to see her. I don't want to see her. I'm afraid. How would she look now?

As Bill drives up the curving entryway to Forest Lawn-Cypress, I spot a dozen cars parked in front of the white, plantation-style mortuary. I realize with a sudden rush of emotion that our friends and relatives are already here, waiting for us.

Bill pulls up behind a huge, gleaming black hearse, and for the first time I see the tiny linen-draped casket in the back window.

I feel a sudden stab. *Oh, God, this is real. Misty, you really are dead!*

Knowing her little body is so near and yet beyond reach or sight wrenches my soul. *I don't want to be here. I don't want to do this. I don't want this to be happening!*

We drive through the huge iron gate, along the winding road in a slow, steady procession—a hearse and a string of automobiles, links in a chain with invisible connections. A strange, somber ritual in a day bursting with warmth and spilling sunshine on lush green grass.

We are here because one tiny baby lived and died.

We stop in a section of the cemetery where only infants are buried. The markers are small, imprinted with little lambs, rabbits, and ducks. We walk to Misty's plot beside a lofty, gnarled old tree.

Dan, Susi's husband, carries the casket to the grave site.

A spray of tiny pink roses, pink and white carnations, and daisies grace the little coffin. Surrounding it are beautiful bouquets and vases of flowers—explosions of color reminding me we are not gathered just to mourn a death but to celebrate life as well.

She is not here. She is not really here.

Misty lives. Elsewhere.

Our family sits in the single row of chairs facing the casket while everyone else—a surprising forty or more people—gather behind us, standing. I'm touched and amazed that so many people have come to pay their respects to a baby they've never seen, whose earthly life amounted to only a couple of hours.

Susi, in a clear, lovely voice ringing with feeling, sings, "Savior, Like a Shepherd Lead Us" and "Through It All."

I weep.

Pastor Wood reads from 2 Samuel 12:16-23. David and Bathsheba's child is dying. David weeps, prays, and fasts for seven days. After the child dies, David rises up, changes his clothes, goes into God's house to worship, then sits down to eat. When his servants question his sudden change in attitude and behavior, David says, "While the child was yet alive, I fasted and wept; for I said, Who can tell whether God will be gracious to me, that the child may live? But now he is dead, why should I fast? Can I bring him back again? I shall go to him, but he shall not return to me."

Pastor Wood points out the blessed hope of the believer, that while our dead child cannot return to us, someday we shall go to be with her. We shall be reunited with Misty in heaven. That knowledge gave David the strength to pick up the pieces of his life and go on; it can be our strength too.

Following Pastor Wood's message and prayer, everyone files by to greet us, give us a warm embrace, tell us they love us. Many have tears in their eyes. I realize they have been crying along with us. I marvel. These people—friends, relatives, acquaintances—have willingly opened themselves to our pain. They are genuinely hurting, literally feeling our grief. I have never felt so loved.

After the service, we return home to a house bustling with activity and bursting with friends and relatives. Several ladies from our Sunday school class are busy in the kitchen serving food—ham, salads, rolls, vegetables, brownies, coffee and tea.

I feel a surprising surge of energy. I have come through the tempest intact, endured the whirlwind. I am still alive, part of the living, surrounded by people who care. They give me energy; they buoy me; their tender words and hugs are a balm to my spirit. I go about the room greeting everyone, stopping to chat, catching up on the latest news. It's been weeks since I've been up and around, gone visiting or to a party. Yes, this could be a party, a family reunion, a festive occasion. I can almost forget why everyone is here.

Evening: The house is quiet. The people have gone; only Mother and Susi are here with us. My friend Vicki drops by briefly, and Bill shows her the slides he just picked up at the photo shop. Pictures of Misty. I am ambivalent about seeing them—eager, yet fearful. The afternoon's sweet conviviality has lulled my emotions.

How will I feel, seeing Misty again, being reminded that she was real?

Vicki looks at the pictures and weeps openly. Mother and Susi refuse to look at all. I look and it all comes back: Misty lying uncovered on a treatment table, barely alive. Misty's sad little face, so pitiful and dear. I remember how warm and smooth her forehead felt when I kissed her, how light and soft she felt in my arms. I do not cry. Baffling: I feel only a peculiar sort of loving detachment.

But I don't fool myself. I sense that another time, another day I will look again and weep bitterly.

Father, I leave the days ahead in Your hands. Thank You for loving us today through so many people, through their cards and phone calls, flowers and plants, meals prepared and tender words spoken. And I praise You, sweet Lord, that when I fall, underneath are the everlasting arms.

THURSDAY, JANUARY 14

I SPEND THE DAY READING a slender little paperback my friend Sally Stuart sent me—Paula D'Arcy's *Song for Sarah*. It's the story of a young mother whose husband and daughter died tragically. It's the saddest book I've ever read. I sob through the entire journal.

I wonder: What is wrong with me that I feel driven to read something so painful just two days after Misty's funeral, a week after her death. It's as if my grief needs something outside itself to focus on, some outside impetus to put the process of mourning in motion all over again, as if by going through the process over and over, I'll begin to get it right and the hurt will start to lessen.

It's like rubbing a sore muscle. It hurts every time you rub it, but it's a good kind of hurt. And when you're through, you feel maybe just a little bit better.

SUNDAY, JANUARY 17

I FEEL AS IF THE PROPS HAVE been knocked out from under me. Mother flew home to Michigan this morning.

During this past month she has given me such constant, loving support in spite of her own physical weaknesses. She was always there for me—my nurse, my comforter, my companion. How will I get along without her?

Already I feel more vulnerable to the pain of losing Misty. While Mother was here, I could shut out the loss to some extent. I was so grateful that the two of us could be together again, whatever the circumstances. Now I feel suddenly alone, an abandoned child.

Still, I go through the motions of an ordinary day. Kim and I clean Heather's room, eat TV dinners, play Uno. But my mind is fragmented. I want to get busy and do things and straighten rooms and work on my writing, but my strength is so fleeting.

As I hang Heather's clothes in her closet, I gaze reluctantly at the tiny dresses she has outgrown—lovely, frilly doll-like things I'd saved for the new baby. Useless now. Misty needed only a little blanket—a pretty, soft knit one Heather never used. It was to have been Misty's receiving blanket. Now I wonder, Why didn't I send a dress and booties to the funeral home too? Why didn't I ask to see her again?

Because no one ever told me I could.

Bill's dad saw Misty the day of the funeral. Yes, my blustery father-in-law, Tony—that squat, gruff Italian with a heart soft as Jello—went to the mortuary early and insisted on seeing his little granddaughter. He got his way.

"How did she look?" I manage to ask.

"Cutest little thing I ever saw," he says with obvious grandfatherly pride.

No other response could please me more.

I envy him his courage. I envy him that last fleeting glimpse. But at least, if I didn't see her, someone did. Her grandfather. We share a special bond now. I'll always remember that he was the last to see her and she was beautiful to him.

Look.

I'm weepy again. Brimming over with sadness. Oh, how I wanted another tiny baby to love, cuddle, and nurse. These motherly instincts and desires that were born anew with Heather, my sweet little toddler, have endured and grown. They are there now, yearning for expression.

I realize they must be redirected. I must accept the fact that there is no child to nurse at my breast. So I take pills to dry up my milk, and I turn my thoughts to Heather, the baby I still have.

Father, my Father, how I thank You for Heather, my darling little whirlwind, just eighteen months old. I am so grateful that You gave her to me before Misty. Now, when I need to feel a baby's arms, there is Heather—still a baby, still in diapers, touting her bottle and her two favorite blankets, jabbering her own special language, so quick and lively, so healthy and intelligent. Such a comfort.

My Jesus, I know it's natural for me to mourn, but I pray that each time the painful waves wash over me, I'll come running to You for wholeness. Meet each bout of grief with Your healing touch.

Thank You, Lord, for the ministering power of Psalm 71. I praise You that every time I call out in despair, You answer back with love and peace.

MONDAY, JANUARY 18

LAST NIGHT I DREAMED OF MISTY. I dreamed I tried to nurse her, even though she was dying. Somehow it was so important to me that she nurse. I think my dream was so vivid because last night I looked again at the slides Bill took of her. It hurt to see Misty's fragile little body lying there, and yet I couldn't take my eyes off her. I'm glad we have these pictures; otherwise I would already be forgetting what she looked like, the frank reality of her.

Another reason for my dream: Last night I watched a TV program on the first American "test tube" baby, showing the actual cesarean delivery of a healthy little five-pound girl. I tried to watch impassively, but I couldn't help thinking that I will likely never again experience the delivery of a whole, healthy child. I don't dare have another baby. I couldn't take on such a risk again. So I grieve for that loss too.

I spend the morning reading a wonderful little book, *Help for Bereaved Parents*, by my writer friend Millie Tengbom. I read and cry, read and cry. She says so much that meets me squarely where I am today. She deals so openly with what happens to a marriage relationship when a child dies.

Most people—myself included—assume that during such a crisis the family pulls together and gives one another the necessary support. I know that for several weeks I've felt disappointed that Bill and I haven't been closer during this trying time. I've felt resentful and angry with him for not being the person I needed him to be. I've even wondered if our marriage would ever be the same.

What a relief to learn from Millie's book that these feelings are natural and even to be expected, that when a child dies it is almost impossible for the husband and wife to meet each other's needs because their own individual needs are so great. Millie revealed an incredible statistic: over 70 percent of all couples separate during the first year after the death of their child!

She says, "The death of a child places a double

load on parents. Each one grieves alone at the same time as each one feels he or she should support the grieving loved one. It is hard both to grieve yourself and support another. Because the death of a child is particularly distressing, tensions enter the marriage relationship and sometimes a new crisis develops."

She also covers another problem area—reestablishing a physical relationship. From couples she interviewed she learned that most husbands want to, most wives don't—for a time at least. I see that ahead as a problem for Bill and me too. Right now, just the thought of a physical union makes me cry. I associate the experience too keenly with the tragedy of Misty. I know I shouldn't, and I don't want to feel that way, but I do. I don't know what it will take for me to overcome these reactions.

I do know that for the last month it has been easier and more comforting for me to be my mother's daughter than to be my husband's wife. Does that make sense? Perhaps I turned automatically to the one who offered solace.

Several times during our ordeal, my brother-in-law Russ looked with sympathy at me and said, "You look like you need to be held." It was his quiet, sincere way of saying I needed comforting. I was touched by his concern because, in truth, I did feel I was lacking comfort and support from Bill. But in retrospect, perhaps I wasn't really seeking out Bill's comfort either. Maybe he felt I wasn't giving him the opportunity. I don't know.

I know that Bill has been more attentive this past week, taking time to rub my back, giving me a spontaneous hug or kiss. And he holds me a few minutes before we fall asleep at night. I want his closeness, and yet I'm wary too, afraid he will want or need or expect more from me than I can give right now.

Help Bill and me, Father, with our individual needs. Help us to draw closer to each other. Help us to remember that we need to make a conscious effort to strengthen our relationship just as we need to make a continuing, conscious effort to remain close to You.

We will try to take it one day at a time . . . loving You.

SATURDAY, JANUARY 23

MY WRITER FRIEND TILL AND I spend the afternoon together working on our writing. As she reads this journal, she mentions Bill's phone call to her early in the morning of January 8th telling her of Misty's birth and death the night before. She says, "I asked him how he was doing, and he said, 'I cried all night.'"

I nearly weep when she tells me that, because I haven't seen Bill cry at all. Maybe I need to see him cry; maybe we need to weep together in each other's arms.

After Till leaves, I tell Bill what she said and he replies noncommittally, "Yeah, I cried some; it was sad." But he won't say any more.

Later I hope we can talk together in bed, but he falls asleep immediately. I lie awake for two hours, crying silently, thinking of all the things I want to say.

We will have to talk sometime, but it's awfully hard to find much privacy in a busy house bustling with a teenager, a preteen, and a toddler. It doesn't help that Bill's an early bird and I'm a night owl. But one of these days we will have to make time to talk. Our relationship has been battered these past two months and it needs mending.

Help us, Lord, to strengthen marital and family ties, so, drawing together, we may bind one another's wounds.

SUNDAY, JANUARY 24

I RETURN TO CHURCH FOR THE first time since going into the hospital with premature labor six weeks ago. It's good to be back. Everyone is so friendly, so sympathetic.

I feel a bond of closeness with these people I've never felt before.

I notice a strange phenomenon. When people come up and speak to me of the baby, it surprises me to see the hurt fresh in their eyes. I feel as if I want to reach out and comfort them because they are hurting for me. I want to say, "Don't feel bad. It's okay."

I feel that way especially while talking with a friend who recently suffered a miscarriage during her third month of pregnancy. She tells me how sorry she is to hear about my baby's death, and adds, "I know my experience was nothing compared with yours."

I disagree with her. "Maybe your situation wasn't as traumatic as mine, but you still lost a child, and that's a deep grief under any circumstances."

She seems to take comfort from my words. Confidentially she says, "It was terrible. I went into a three-month depression after my miscarriage."

I'm touched that this casual friend chooses to share her pain with me. I sense that I am building emotional bonds with people I've known for years just in passing, tender ties of empathy and compassion that never would have formed had it not been for Misty.

After church we drive to the cemetery to see the spot where Misty is buried. There is nothing that speaks of her here, no marker yet, only grass and sunshine and a caressing breeze. Heather runs gleefully across the vast expanse of grass, opening her arms wide, as if catching the wonder of a sweet-smelling earth and glorious sky. Her laughter soars on the wings of the wind. I stand at my baby's grave site and watch my other baby run free, boundless and brimming with joy, and am reminded again of the curious juxtaposition of death and life.

MONDAY, JANUARY 25

THEY SAY IT'S NATURAL TO FEEL depressed when your child dies.

Am I depressed?

How do I recognize it?

Does it have a name?

Is it the same as sorrow? I know what sorrow feels like. I'm not sure about depression.

I don't think I'm depressed.

Does that mean it's still to come? I hope not.

Grief seems so unpredictable. It's not a once-and-for-all cry or scream; it doesn't hit all at once and then go away. No, it seems to come in bits and pieces, hitting unexpectedly, stealing in unawares. It ebbs and flows like the tide, a sudden sadness washing over me like the sea, startling, biting, unearthing buried memories, then receding, like water into sand.

Lord, is it the circumstances of Misty's brief life—because You let me know You would be taking her home to Yourself while she still lived within me—that keep me from grieving more deeply? I'm sure if I'd lost Kim or David or Heather my pain would be nearly unbearable. But with Misty, it's as if her life were set aside for You even before I knew her, surely long before I ever saw her. I feel such a strong sense of Your purpose and plan in her fragile, fleeting life. I believe You have touched many people already through her. I know You are touching me.

Help me to grow through this experience in compassion and tenderness; don't let the Devil use Misty's life and death as a tool of bitterness or contention or depression. Don't give him an inch of victory in this.

Father, when I am alone and sad, I sing hymns until I feel like praising You again. Hymns work wonders. They comfort me and help me praise You, Lord, when I might otherwise start to question or feel sorry for myself. They focus my attention instead on You, my Savior, lover of my soul.

TUESDAY, JANUARY 26

I'M READING THE BOOK SHEILA gave me—Edith Schaeffer's *Affliction*. Mrs. Schaeffer points out that it's sin and Satan that are responsible for the tribulation and pain and death in our world. Not God. It wasn't God's will for us to experience such terrible heartaches and sorrows; He wanted only good things for us—life and love and joy. But when Adam and Eve gave in to the Devil's temptation, they made a deliberate choice that opened the door to evil and pain and death.

I wonder: Why do we have such a hard time putting the blame where it belongs?

THURSDAY, JANUARY 28

TODAY I'M DEPRESSED. NO ONE *has to tell me its name. I recognize its face and I abhor it. God, I don't want to be depressed!*

At 1 P.M. I have my postpartum checkup with Dr. Anzaldo. Bill takes me. Dr. Anzaldo talks with us about the risks involved in having another child.

Because of the chromosome problem with Misty, the risk in future pregnancies is greatly increased—one chance in twenty of another chromosome defect, compared with one chance in seventy-five for other women my age.

Dr. Anzaldo tries to say it kindly, but his words come out blunt and hard-hitting: "The next child could have similar critical abnormalities and yet live forty or fifty years."

I feel stunned, devastated. His words sting like a physical blow. Apparently he reads my horrified expression because, in spite of his dire warning, he adds, "Go ahead and have another child if you want one—but have the amniocentesis." He doesn't finish the idea, but I know what he means. If there's a chromosome problem, I can choose to have an abortion.

I remind him that that's not an option for me. I don't believe in abortion.

"In that case," he says seriously, "it would be better for you not to have any more children."

I nod agreement, but the finality of his words stirs something deep and primal within me. No more children. No more pregnancies. I knew it before, but now it is official. The doctor has spoken. No more babies . . . unless abortion is an option.

I feel shaken. Once again, just as when I decided not to use the IUD, my convictions must go from the theoretical to the personal: If I could condone abortion I could consider having another child.

But for me there is no room for argument. To accept the option of abortion would mean uprooting my most basic, instinctive feelings about the relationship between God and human life. I could no more tear out those convictions than I could cast away my faith in Christ—not even for the chance to have the baby I so desire.

Before my appointment with Dr. Anzaldo concludes, I work up the courage to ask another question pressing on my mind. "Who is responsible for a condition like Misty's—the mother or the father?"

Dr. Anzaldo's answer is direct. "It's the mother's egg that causes most, if not all, chromosome defects in offspring."

My voice catches as I tell him, "I don't understand. Would you explain it to us?"

He meets my gaze and says gently, "You see, while the male's sperm are constantly being created fresh over the years, every egg the mother will ever have is already in her body at birth. As the mother ages, so do her eggs, increasing the chance of a defective egg being fertilized."

I feel stunned. There it is. My fault. Bill could have had a normal child if it weren't for my defective egg. Somehow I had assumed that because I was still in my thirties, I was safe. Not so. I feel a sudden, undeniable measure of guilt, realizing I'm the one responsible for Misty's condition.

But then Christ's Spirit moves within, reminding me, *If Misty had never been conceived, there wouldn't be that unique little being in heaven today. She lives. You gave her life. God gave her wholeness.*

Yes. Hold on to that. *God, help me see it through Your eyes!*

I leave Dr. Anzaldo's office feeling shaken, fighting dismay. How can I emotionally accept the fact that I can never have more children? I already mourn Misty's death. Must I also mourn that part of my life involving pregnancy, childbirth, and a newborn, nursing infant?

I knew it rationally before. Why is it hitting my emotions so hard now? It's the finality. The door slammed shut on one of the most cherished and significant dimensions of my life. I thrived on being pregnant, feeling new life moving within me, nursing and nurturing a newborn baby. Those maternal feelings are still there, crying for expression. What do I do with them? How do I make them go away?

MONDAY, FEBRUARY 1

A BUSY MORNING—getting the crew off to work and school, chasing after Heather, washing clothes, managing a quiet time of prayer while Heather naps, and, with doctor's permission, trying a few awkward exercises for the first time in months.

Last week Charette Kvernstoen invited me to teach fiction at the *Decision* School of Christian Writing in Minneapolis this coming August. It's the nudge I need to convince me I still have a ministry in teaching.

Three years ago, shortly before I became pregnant with Heather, I sensed that the Lord was leading me to focus my attention more on home and family. As God worked in my heart, I welcomed the chance to put aside books and get back to babies. But now, thanks to Charette's invitation, I think God is showing me it's time to get back to the books—and teaching.

THURSDAY, FEBRUARY 11

Susi telephones with incredible news: She's pregnant!

My sister Susi, a talented singer and ventriloquist known professionally as Susan Gift Porter, has performed Christian family concerts across the country and delighted thousands of children and adults for many years. Yet the one thing she has yearned for most has eluded her—a child of her own.

For four long years we have prayed that she would conceive a child, but it didn't happen. She and Dan had nearly accepted the fact that theirs would be a childless marriage. But now—now God is sending them a new life, their very own baby.

Susi adds a startling footnote: Her baby was conceived the very week that Misty died.

SATURDAY, FEBRUARY 13

Susi and dan come for dinner. When they speak of their baby, they are like two children at Christmas— incredulous, mystified, excited, unsettled. Already they are seeing the trappings and accouterments of parenthood through new eyes. Suddenly Susi is interested in talking about Lamaze and layettes and maternity fashions and midnight feedings—all the things I've probably bored her with all these years.

I can't miss the irony of our situation. Throughout my pregnancies for both Heather and Misty, I prayed that Susi would be able to share that special joy with me through a baby of her own. I felt almost guilty expecting my fourth child when she seemed unable to have even one. Now I feel like a relay runner who must hand the baton on to the next runner and sit out the rest of the race.

I admit to a certain bittersweet pain. I am over-joyed for Susi, yet my own loss is underscored. It is such a peculiar, mixed reaction, this keen joy and inter-mingled ache.

After dinner, Bill and I give Susi and Dan all the baby paraphernalia and clothing Heather has out-grown—infant seat, walker, baby swing and scales, plus a carton of tiny baby dresses, gowns, and kimonos I had packed away for our new baby.

I can tell that these commonplace items Susi and Dan have seen a dozen times before take on a sparkling new significance as they picture them for their own child. Bill and I exchange a wistful glance. I know he feels what I'm feeling. It's as if we're bestowing a spe-cial treasure, sharing some of the love and warmth and promise these items represent.

Eagerly I go about the house collecting all my books and magazines on pregnancy, childbirth, and baby care and present them to Susi. I bask in her sud-den, intense interest in all the maternal things that have absorbed my attention for well over a decade.

All our conversation this evening is about pregnan-cy and babies. Bill and I delight in giving advice and recounting some of our own experiences as parents.

Susi wants to know: "What should I eat? How should I feel? What should I do?"

When I show Dan a picture and description of an embryo at one month, he exclaims in awe, "Is all that happening already?"

Yes, Dan, I muse silently, *all that and more. The miracle is so great. There's so much to marvel at and enjoy.*

How I look forward to sharing this special time with Susi. Pregnancy and childbirth are still so fresh in my own life, so close to the core of my own emotions, so vitally a part of my being. But I marvel—and I suppose I will not stop marveling—over this ambivalence I feel—elation swathed in pain, gain and loss in a single swell of emotion.

Lord, I thank You for answered prayer, that while the answer for me during this last pregnancy was no, the answer for my sister, after so many years, is yes!

Deliver me, Jesus, from envy or jealousy. You know how much I want a baby for Susi, but You know, too, how her pregnancy scratches at a wound that has just begun to heal. Help me to dwell on the joy I feel for her. Watch over her. Bless her baby. And love us all, Lord Jesus, through one another.

SUNDAY, FEBRUARY 14

WE'RE REALLY BLOWING IT TODAY. Bill's angry, I'm depressed, Kim's sick, David's sad, and Heather is acting like a holy terror. She's screeching even as I write this.

This is supposed to be a pleasant Valentine's Sunday, but it's anything but. We were all in the car ready to go to church this morning when the engine wouldn't start, an all-too-familiar occurrence lately. In fact, our car has broken down every day this week. Bill has repeatedly taken it into the shop or had it towed in, and each day he has picked it up with high hopes that it will run. But inevitably it sputters and stalls, or never starts at all.

It was a miracle Heather and I didn't get killed on Tuesday when I drove in the rain to pick Kim up at school. The car stalled again and again in the middle of a busy intersection while irritated drivers whizzed on around me.

When the car refused to start again this morning, it was the last straw for Bill. I doubt if anything makes him more upset than a car that won't run—especially since it's the only automobile we own.

Bill took two days of vacation time this week to run errands, and the car failed him both days. We had such pleasant plans for today—a get-together with friends from Sunday school—but we've had to cancel. Both Kim and David are due at the orthodontist's office tomorrow. We don't know how they'll get there, or how Bill will get the car into the shop to be fixed, or how he'll get to work.

We're all frustrated, angry. Anyone for screaming?

Lord, we have such small reserves of strength. Why must so many needless, hapless incidents drag us down? With such persistent irritations, our spirits become bone-dry, and we have nothing left to give one another.

It's a chain reaction: The car won't start; Bill becomes frustrated and angry; I become depressed; Kim and David grow restive or sullen or irritated; and Heather expresses the sum total of our communal misery in one long, nerve-wracking squall.

Our defenses are paper-thin lately, Father. We all need Your restoring touch. Bill needs to know You are there for him; he feels the burden of so many responsibilities. Things like cars that won't start and bills piling up and a savings account nearly scraped clean test his endurance almost to the breaking point.

Those things bother me too, but what bothers me even more is the way these things upset him. Yet I know it's wrong of me to meet his frustrations with my own frustration.

Lord, help me to drink afresh of Your living waters— Your renewing Spirit—so that I will not come empty-handed or cold-hearted to Bill when he needs me. Let my heart be tender and my arms open so that You can love him through me.

TUESDAY, FEBRUARY 16

LORD, I'M REALLY DEPRESSED TODAY. *It's been nearly six weeks now since Misty came and went so swiftly. Sometimes I think it gets harder just when people assume it's getting easier.*

Now, when the solicitous cards and calls have stopped coming and friends have stopped asking how I'm feeling, now I feel hard, cold reality settling in permanently. There is no baby. There won't be any baby. I'm reminded of that fact painfully every time I see a pregnant woman or a newborn infant. The bitter fact of it slaps me like cold water, stings like a needle in the arm—a sudden, unexpected twinge.

I feel it today when I open an advertising circular that begins, "Congratulations on your new baby. . . ," and again when I stare at the doctors' statements, ultrasound claims, and hospital bills that have poured in. I feel angry. Silently I scream, Why should we have to pay so much when we didn't even get to bring home a baby!

WEDNESDAY, FEBRUARY 17

MY DEPRESSION LIFTS THIS MORNING as I sit and hold Heather in my arms, rocking her and singing hymns. I talk aloud to God, unburdening my heart. Heather nestles against me, listening curiously, or chatters back amiably, apparently content in my contentment.

I realize: I need to talk aloud to the Lord every day. Prayers in my head won't do it for me. I need to speak the words, make them concrete, audible, a regular conversation with Jesus. Otherwise, prayers become a ritual for me—lengthy thought-prayers, I mean; the sentences are never quite formed, and the needs remain fuzzy, and I fall asleep mentally.

Of course, brief prayers are another thing. All day

long I shoot up thought-prayers in response to what's happening around me. Those prayers are like breathing—spontaneous and natural. I couldn't live spiritually without them.

What I'm saying is that I need both kinds of prayer to survive—the frequent silent moments as well as the leisurely audible conversations.

Lord, my depression of the past few days reminds me of my daily dependence on You. When I move even a little away from your presence, the light dims and I feel as if I'm having to go it alone. I need to talk with You daily, to allow Your presence and Word to wash me regularly. Father, the more we share, the more I see things through Your eyes; and the more my heart and mind dwell upon You, the more I feel of Your attributes within me—love, joy, peace, forgiveness, patience.

My problem is that I take You for granted. Sometimes I allow days to pile up without our time together. I neglect You, go it alone, or toss up brief prayer missiles that miss their mark. I treat You like a filling station. I come to You and fill up on Your Spirit, then go my way until I run out of gas and have to push myself back for a refill. I wouldn't have such ups and downs if I'd stay close to the source of Your power. Forgive me, Lord. I know what in-depth times with You are like—the communion, the harmony, the oneness of our spirits. So it is all the more lamentable when I don't zealously pursue them.

Father, You are faithful even when I don't give You my time and devotion. Our times apart are my losses. I take such comfort and joy in Your presence, one would think I would jealously guard those precious times every day. Lord, help me to keep all systems open in my prayer life, so depression won't stall the engine and require a major overhaul somewhere down the line.

MONDAY, FEBRUARY 22

THIS IS THE WEEK OF MY ORIGINAL due date, the week Misty was scheduled to be born. Instead, it seems like years since her birth and death.

These past few days have been bittersweet. At times I feel a pang of anguish, of sadness or yearning, but more often I feel an inner energy that buoys me through the day's activities. It's Christ's energy, His Spirit upholding me.

I savor my common treasures—the lamplight catching Bill's strong features just so; the gracefulness of my daughter Kim as she pirouettes about the house in her own make-believe ballet; my son David's lanky good looks and his earnestness when he whispers, "I love you, Mom"; and my lively little Heather—all baby and bounce and bombast and bluff.

Jesus, my blessed provider! Death has rent my heart and left a hole in my life, but You are mending me and filling this vacuum of loss with a brand-new tenderness and fresh appreciation for this lovely, baffling, multihued crazy quilt called life. I am more inclined lately to savor the subtle tastes and textures of my mundane days, having been reminded jarringly that there is nothing ordinary about life, that it is too tenuous, too fragile, too brief to be taken for granted.

Lord, You've given me a keen sense of gratitude for all that I still hold in my hands—my family, my home, my health, my writing. My sense of purpose and meaning in life has not dimmed; I am as convinced as ever of Your loving, blessed control over all the events of my life.

WEDNESDAY, FEBRUARY 24

FURY.
   Hot blood rage.

81

Fuming . . . boiling . . . exploding . . . spilling bile . . .
Oh, God, I'm so angry I can hardly write this. I want
to throw something or pound something or yell or break
something into smithereens.

Lord, I know I should accept all You bring into my life
as Your perfect will, and haven't I been doing that fairly
well? If You're going to make the big things go wrong, can't
You at least let the little things go right? Do I have to smile
and accept everything graciously and say it's all right when
it's not?

Why is it that the little disappointments make the big
ones harder to take?

I just got back a short story manuscript from an
editor who kept it seven months and who just last week
assured me she was 99 percent sure she would be using
it. Now back it comes, with the feeble explanation that
the editorial board decided on another article at the last
minute.

Sorry about the bad news, she says. I want to
shout back, *My baby just died and I need some good news*
around here!

Why does each new thing always lead back to the
other?

I want to comprehend logically why I'm so angry
and why this rejection letter hits me so hard. After all,
I've received hundreds of rejection slips during my
twelve years of writing professionally, so why is this one
so devastating?

I realize: My writing career is extremely important
to me, and now, more than ever, I need to see evidence
of success in it. I need to feel that I'm accomplishing
something. I need some sort of positive feedback to
offset my sense of loss over Misty.

Maybe I feel so stricken because I pour myself into
my writing, laboriously, word upon word, just as I
poured myself into Misty, creating her cell by cell. She

came out all wrong. She didn't have a chance. Now, somehow I'm reminded of that fact by a rejected manuscript.

God knows I need to do something right. I need to know that what I'm creating will be accepted. Even this journal. For me this journal *is* Misty. What if it's not accepted?

Father, I know I will see these things from Your point of view again, maybe even in the next hour. But right now, at this moment, all I feel like doing is crying. I know in my head that if You strip me of all that is vital to me, I will realize that the only important thing—the only important One—is You. But please, don't ask me to be rational just yet. For a few minutes more, let me cry.

Lord, it's evening now and I'm ready to see things Your way. I realize that this incident today was a nudge from You, reminding me that I am to find my solace and satisfaction in You alone. When I look to any source besides You to meet my needs, I stumble. Or I fall flat on my face, as I did today.

I know You have given me my writing career as a means of ministering to others and serving You. When it becomes too consuming a need, or my preoccupation, then I am misusing it. Forgive me, Jesus. Keep my eyes steadfastly on You.

Lord, I recognize, too, that my anger today wasn't just in response to a rejected manuscript; it was my grief over Misty erupting in another unexpected way. It's just like when Bill exploded over the car constantly breaking down; then he mentioned Misty, and we both knew she was on his mind through the whole thing.

Why must grief be so paradoxical, so sly, stalking us, springing from dark corners and minor disappointments, mushrooming out of silly irritations and fatigue, gnashing at our dwindling defenses? Why can't we pin it down, this phantasmagoria called grief? Why can't we look it in the eye, grip it hard in our hands, shake it, rend it, and cast it aside for good?

Father, my Father, I run weary and spent back into Your arms. Carry me high so my feet won't drag. I may not always show it, but I love You.

SATURDAY, MARCH 6

TODAY OUR FAMILY GOES TO the mortuary to select a grave marker for Misty. Most of the plaques are large and cold and forbidding, but we choose a small one with tiny, frolicking animals gracing the corners.

While Bill and I fill out the necessary forms, Heather toddles about the room, shattering the formal, imposed stillness with her squeals. She ducks behind the mahogany desk and unabashedly plays peek-a-boo with Kim and David. As we leave, she tries to pick a flower from someone's funeral bouquet. Not for an instant does the austerity and imperiousness of this place squelch her crowing, audacious *joie de vivre.*

Thank You, Lord Jesus, for Misty—for the extra measure of tenderness and sensitivity her wisp of memory will prompt in us for the rest of our lives.

And thank You for Heather, our counterpoint of joy, who keeps us ever mindful of the precious, profound balance between death and life.

THURSDAY, MARCH 11

I'M READING VORACIOUSLY—everything from Marjorie Holmes to weighty, plodding books on genetics and heredity. I have a seemingly insatiable hunger to learn all I can about Misty's condition and the whole chromosome conundrum that results in such ill-fated children.

I've found almost nothing on Misty's specific genetic anomaly (three chromosomes on #18, or trisomy 18), but I've read enough to marvel that any of us ever comes out whole with all systems go. I stand in awe of my three normal, healthy children. What a miracle that their chromosomes—those myriad invisible essences that spell life—came together in just the right way.

I'm also reading some very helpful and comforting books for bereaved parents: *After a Loss in Pregnancy* and *Coping with Tragedy: Successfully Facing the Problem of a Seriously Ill Child.* Realizing what Misty would have been had she lived, my compassion for parents with retarded or defective children has expanded enormously. I identify achingly with them, knowing how close Bill and I came to raising such a child.

SUNDAY, MARCH 14

A MISERABLE DAY. OUR CAR BREAKS down again just as we try to go to church. Bill is outraged. For months now he has spent his time, money, and energy trying to restore that automobile to running order. More times than we can count we've faced the inconveniences and logistical problems of living without transportation. Bill has felt helpless, baffled, perhaps even emasculated by a ridiculous—but indispensable—piece of machinery.

I find myself wondering, Can something as ordinary and prosaic as an automobile cause a man to have a nervous breakdown and shred the peace and stability of his family? The question isn't totally conjectural. I don't dare voice another concern, the submerged, accusatory question: *If I can cope with our baby's death, why can't you cope with a broken automobile?*

I sense the destructiveness and futility of such a question, and I sense that the annoyances and vexations we are both experiencing now may be tentacles of a greater, enduring desolation—our sense of loss and helplessness over Misty's death. So I will try to tread cautiously, humbly around my husband's shortcomings in the hopes that he will walk as carefully around mine.

TUESDAY, MARCH 23

THINGS ARE BETTER LATELY. For a change, the pluses outnumber the minuses. Our car is working again. The tensions in our household have eased. We're having family devotions again with the children, not every day, but as often as time and busy, conflicting schedules permit.

And for me personally, several pluses: An invitation to teach at Forest Home's School of Christian Writing in June; my novel *Kara* on Bethany's best sellers list again; and happily, a return to my writing, as time and Heather permit—penning a poem about Misty and editing this journal with my writer friends Till and Sheila.

WEDNESDAY, MARCH 24

Oh, Lord, how variegated have been the colors
and textures of our days.
Some smooth and sun-washed;
others dead-end dreary and suffocating as a cave.
Some days I find myself moving effortlessly
through the clear waters of Your will.
I breathe You in,
see through Your eyes,
meet the ripples and waves head-on,
straight and steady, a seasoned craft.
I sail goal-clear toward the horizon,
Your master plan unfailingly before me.
But other days I capsize and flounder,
trying to go it alone.
My arms flail, my head spins.
I sink.
I take in great gulps of self-pity.

I nearly drown within myself,
collapsing, shipwrecked, on my own feckless,
hastily erected defenses.
Frustrations seek to obliterate faith;
the master plan blurs, becomes inscrutable.
No earth-shaking crises, these importune incidents
that ravage my days.
Little things—stone upon stone,
pebbles in the shoe,
irritants of the soul.
Scrutinized impassively, one by one,
they shrink, become minuscule, tolerable.
They dissolve like salt on the tongue.
But I can't always be impassive, or objective,
or generous of spirit.
Not when I'm hurting.
Instead, my mind turns shrewish,
my tone grows shrill.
My nerves become high tension wires.
I wonder, with almost an obsessive urgency,
Why do minor problems take on such major
    proportions?
Why do the concerns that ride the periphery of our
    lives
jam the spokes and nearly split the hub?
I'm not complaining, Father.
Actually,
I'm asking forgiveness.
My days don't have to be multihued—
a chiaroscuro blend of darks and lights;
they could all be bright, Son-washed days,
if I depended more on You.
But I'm doing better.
All of us—better.
The good days outnumber the bad.
Normalcy returns inch by priceless inch,
hour by hour, granting us again
the quiet bliss of comfortable routine.

Lord, help both Bill and me
to communicate more with You
and with each other.
Help us to listen not only to each other's words,
but let us hear with compassion the hidden
  message,
the nameless, aching, unspoken cries of the heart.
We will be all right, Father.
Most of the time I'm convinced of it.
But, Lord, when the days are fractured,
redeem them.
And me.
I can't do it alone, Jesus,
even though sometimes
I act as if I can.

THURSDAY, MARCH 25

BILL'S SISTER ANNETTE TELEPHONES, near tears, with an urgent prayer request for her pastor's family: This afternoon Pastor Jon's wife Anne found their three-year-old son drowning in the backyard swimming pool. Anne rescued him, performed CPR, then rushed the unconscious youngster to the hospital.

"What are the boy's chances?" I ask.

"The doctors induced a coma to lower his body temperature. They hope they can revive him after seventy-two hours." In stricken tones, Annette adds, "He shows no brain waves."

For the rest of the day, this child I do not know preys upon my mind. Somehow I have a stake in his life. He has to live; he has to make it.

Please, oh, God, let him be all right!

FRIDAY, MARCH 26

ANNETTE TELEPHONES AND TELLS ME brokenly, "Pastor Jon's little boy—Charlie—his name was Charlie—he died without regaining consciousness."

No.
Yes.
It can't be.
It's so.

After I hang up the phone, I begin to weep—can't stop weeping—sobbing now—for Charlie—for Charlie's parents—for me. Pain bitter as gall spills inside me. I'm shooting back down the tunnel—back into darkness—grief rising up over my head, engulfing me.

God, I can't cope with children dying!

TUESDAY, MARCH 30

A NNETTE INVITES ME TO ATTEND Charlie's funeral with her today. I consider going, then decide against it. I can't do it. I would be subjecting myself to an ordeal I'm not sure I can handle—going through the motions—and emotions—of another child's funeral. In my heart I would be reliving Misty's death and burial. It's too soon for that; the wound is still too tender.

So, instead, I sit alone in my room and write a poem for Pastor Jon and Anne McNeff, Charlie's parents, a prayer expressing much more than I could put into words were we to meet and talk face to face.

FOR CHARLIE'S PARENTS

A little boy died last week—
a bubbly, bright-eyed, three-year-old blond.
Leaving his lunch on the kitchen table,
he slipped outside
and opened the gate
drawn to the shimmering water.
He drowned in the family swimming pool
at his parents' new home
in a nicer neighborhood
that was to be safer
for their daughter to walk to school.

The child's mother found him
and retrieved him,
her fear as ice-gripping
as the late-winter water.
She labored to breathe
her own life into him
while his sister
watched and screamed,
Don't die, Charlie!
Don't die!
But he did.
I cried when I heard about Charlie.
My heart ached for his parents
whose faces I can't even recall.
But I feel with them
as if we were family.
I wanted to go to the funeral today
but it's too soon after Misty
too soon to follow the same winding road
of that familiar cemetery
past the freshly turned earth
where my daughter lies,
to another child's grave.
So I stayed home and prayed,
prayed for strength for the family
to face this hour
and the harder ones to come.
Dear God, don't let Charlie's parents
be ashamed of their pain
or think it makes them
any less Christian.
Let them know it's all right
at times
to be angry,
to want to blame someone—
even You.
Help them to remember You love Charlie
even more than they.

Save them from the useless
unproductive *what ifs*
remembering that *what is*
has been filtered through
Your perfect plan for Your own.
Free them from guilt—
the natural tendency to blame themselves
or each other.
Remind them that nothing
either of them did
or didn't do
could have changed
what was in
Your preordained
scheme of things.
Even so,
You, holy God,
did not extinguish Charle's life.
You simply threw open heaven's doors
spread your arms
and welcomed him with a hug
no three-year-old could resist.
When their own arms feel empty
help his parents see him
safe with You—
not gone,
no less a person,
just somewhere else—
a boy so quick and eager
he ran on home ahead of them.
Lord, help Charlie's parents
understand how hard it is
for mates to offer comfort
when each is hurting.
Don't let them expect
too much of each other.
Let them be patient
when their partner

needs to talk
or cry or be silent.
Help them to remember
each person heals
in a different way
at a different pace.
Let them rejoice in the good days
when the pain seems diminished
and the future bright.
Deliver them from depression
during the bad days
when the hurt washes back
stunning them with its power.
Give them a quiet understanding
of the peculiar ways of grief—
how it ebbs and flows,
striking suddenly,
unexpectedly,
then abating,
biding its time,
reasserting itself
just when one thinks
it's gone for good.
There's nothing wrong with mourning.
It's natural,
necessary for healing.
It's a process that polishes
or tarnishes
the soul,
depending on what one
chooses
to do with it.
Some become bitter.
But, dear God,
make Charlie's parents
better and brighter
and even more beautiful
through their pain.

And love them abundantly
through all of us
who care
more than we can say.

SUNDAY, APRIL 11

Eᴀsᴛᴇʀ: ᴀ ʙʟᴇssᴇᴅ, ʙɪᴛᴛᴇʀsᴡᴇᴇᴛ ᴅᴀʏ. From the time I awake this morning I feel on the verge of tears. I can't stop thinking about Misty.

Before church we drive to the cemetery. It hasn't occurred to me until now to put flowers on Misty's grave. I've always mildly scoffed at the idea of decorating graves with Christmas wreaths and plastic trees or Easter baskets. I always assumed that people who lavished such garish endearments on a little plot of ground must be either living in the past or refusing to face reality.

But on this sunless, rain-soaked Easter morning, as we pull off the road beside that familiar spot, I find myself wincing at the thought of approaching Misty's unmarked plot empty-handed. How I long to bring some offering, a token of our attachment, of our once-oneness, not so much for her sake as for ours—a ritual of our belonging, confirming that Misty is still indeed a link in our family circle, albeit a displaced link.

Or should I say, *we* are the displaced ones, waiting to be claimed by heaven?

I am surprised by the intensity of my desire to bestow some memorial on Misty's grave. But it's too late to bring anything this morning. It has been a tight week for us financially. Bill and I don't have enough cash between us even to purchase a cheap grocery store lily.

So I keep my yearnings to myself, silently imagining how it might have been had the children and I gathered frivolous treasures from Easters past for a basket for Misty. The gesture might have provided an opportunity to share together in a special endeavor of

93

love. We might even have touched our secret places of pain and our tucked-away dreams for their tiny, absent sister.

What do they think and feel about Misty? I never ask. They never say.

I haven't reached the conclusion that it's necessary to decorate graves for every occasion—or *any* occasion. But I do understand now why some people feel motivated to do so. As Bill and I walk through the cemetery observing the fresh, lovingly placed bouquets, the plastic baskets, the pink rabbits and painted eggs, I feel none of the condescension I once might have felt.

Instead, I sympathize wholeheartedly. I feel a sense of awe and painful respect for these parents who still decorate the graves of infants born the same year as my oldest daughter. Their babies would have been fourteen now, like Kim; bright, effervescent teenagers, like my Kim.

These mothers and fathers who bring their gifts to weather-beaten graves carry with them their visions of what might have been. I know these faithful, unforgetting parents now. I understand. I am in their skin. I am one of them.

Leaving the cemetery, we drive directly to church. Throughout the worship service my preoccupation with Misty remains. I fight back tears as we sing, "Christ the Lord Is Risen Today." Then Pastor Borror's message grips my emotions with startling force as he tells this story to illustrate the vastness of heaven to the human mind:

Imagine a little fetus in the womb, warm, safe, listening contentedly to his mother's heartbeat. Suppose you could say, "Little baby, soon you're going to be born. Isn't that wonderful?"

Baby might reply, "What's 'being born'?"

You'd say, "It means living and breathing and

walking and talking and being with people who love you."

"Will it hurt?"

"Maybe a little, for a short time, but you won't even remember it."

The little fetus might insist, "I'm happy where I am. I don't want to leave this nice safe place. It's warm and snug. It's all I know."

And you'd reply, "But, little baby, you don't understand. There's so much in this world for you to see and hear and touch and taste and experience. There's something called sky, and the sun, and clouds, and oceans, and flowers, and trees. There's food to eat and places to see and things to do. There's a mother's kiss and a father's embrace, a bird's sweet song and a kitten's soft fur. There are smiles and smells and swings and stars—"

And then you'd stop in frustration, for how can you describe night and day and summer and winter and music and love and all the other beautiful things this world contains to someone who has never experienced them?

So it is when God tries to give us a picture of heaven.

As Dr. Borror shares his illustration of the unborn baby, in my mind I envision our own little Misty leaving the dark confines of the womb, pausing briefly in this unfamiliar earth-world, then hurrying on to heaven to experience a beauty and glory and joy that remain incomprehensible to me.

I marvel as I realize that, even after my twenty-seven years as a Christian, I still see and experience Christ "through a glass darkly." But my tiny, helpless, ill-formed baby now stands in God's presence and sees Him with perfect sight and basks whole and glad and beautiful in His glorious light and love.

Evening: After a delicious dinner at Annette's, our two families attend the Easter cantata at her church. I know Pastor Jon and his wife Anne have probably received my poem about their son Charlie, and now I want to tell them of my caring face-to-face.

Anne, a captivating young woman with the fresh, natural beauty of a teenager, comes over immediately and thanks me for the poem. "I cried and cried," she says. "I know you know the pain."

After church, in the vestibule, Bill and I meet Pastor Jon, a tall, strapping brunette with a mustache. While others mill about, exchanging Easter greetings, the three of us open our hearts and unabashedly share our feelings.

"I read your poem before Anne did," he says. "I told her, 'Honey, you'd better sit down before you read this.'"

As we talk, we agree how vital and comforting are the expressions of love and sympathy from others. "I got so I didn't even read the printed verses on cards," he tells me. "I went straight to the personal, hand-written messages and devoured them."

I nod, adding, "I felt as if Jesus were loving me in a brand-new way through other people. It was unlike anything I ever experienced before."

I sense that we could talk for hours, kin of a rare and hurting kind. But there is a joy in our sharing too—an exclamation of Christ's power to keep and console, mingled with the mutual bittersweet empathy of heart-torn survivors.

Afterward I reflect, This is just one of the reasons God permitted Misty's death—that Bill and I might minister to Pastor Jon and Anne just as the two of them will minister to others who grieve over the loss of a child, a parent, a friend.

There is a beauty and joy in grief that is the other side of pain. I see it now. But it's up to each individual to flip the coin and call out which side wins.

Father, I began this day absorbed once again by the pain of loss. I remembered that, months ago, I looked forward to this Easter Sunday when I would have a beautiful new baby to dress up and carry in my arms to church. Instead, my arms were empty on this morning that stands for life and new beginnings. Our Easter celebration began with a solemn trek to the cemetery.

But You, my Savior, met me today in a special way. You ministered through two others who also grieve over their child's death and yet rejoice in You. Through them You allowed me to comfort and be comforted.

I praise You for this resurrection Sunday and the assurance of life beyond death. I praise You, holy God, who became sin for us, who, being the fountain of life, tasted death and swallowed it for us. Because of You, death is no longer the fence that bars us from heaven, but the open door that takes us home to You.

I praise You that joy is not dependent on circumstances, that joy at times soars better and brighter over dark, troubled waters than over calm and pleasant seas.

WEDNESDAY, APRIL 21

HOW IMPORTANT FRIENDSHIPS are to me lately! What a balm they are to a hurting heart. For me, for many years, friends have seemed more a luxury than a necessity. Now, more and more they are becoming essential.

Strange. I, who have always been naturally shy and reserved, now feel compelled to reach out to those around me in a bolder, more personal way. I find myself wanting to claim acquaintances as friends and desiring to draw my friends into the confidential, seldom-frequented circle of my life.

I'm writing letters to people I haven't corresponded with in months or years. I look forward eagerly, sometimes almost urgently, to spending time with Sheila or Till. I covet our special moments together, whether they be lunches out, shopping sprees, bookstore browsings, leisurely telephone conversations, or productive writing critique sessions.

I love with a freer, unguarded compassion those who have walked with me through these past shadowed months. Now as never before I want to share with these faithful friends, to express what we really feel. I want to be able to touch their hurts and help them as they have helped me.

I realize: All of us are hurting in one way or another. I am aware of that fact more all the time. I sensed it before, but I was wary of touching another's wound, of taking on another's pain. I was afraid of being clumsy and helpless in the face of grief. Because I couldn't find the perfect words to offer someone who hurt, I often said nothing at all.

Now I know that the words aren't important; the love and the caring are. Being there is what counts; being available, being a friend, even when there are no words, no answers, no pat solutions. I want to be a friend; I want to be someone others can turn to with their losses and needs. Because of Misty, my arms are open wider than before.

THURSDAY, MAY 6

WHILE READING THE NEWSPAPER, I come across a Letter to the Editor from a new mother. She praises her obstetrician for his helpfulness and solicitude during her pregnancy and childbirth. I'm startled to see the name of my own obstetrician, Dr. Carl Natter.

Unexpectedly, memories of my last conversation with Dr. Natter come flooding back, especially his sober tone when he told me over the phone, "It looks like there's a problem with the baby, Carole."

A problem with the baby!

At the time I didn't realize the import of his words, nor was I aware that he had already transferred me to a high-risk pregnancy specialist at another hospital. Just like that, with a simple phone call, the direction of my life was altered.

Now, as I read the new mother's letter in today's newspaper, I can't help thinking, *If things had been different, I might have written that letter . . .*

FRIDAY, MAY 7

An anniversary of sorts: Four months ago today Misty died.

Sheila and I get together for lunch. Afterward, as we go over the latest entry in this journal, I start to cry. I don't want to. I feel the tears mounting and fight them back in vain. I feel foolish. I've worked before on this journal with both Sheila and Till, always without tears. So why now?

Perhaps because Misty would have been four months old today? Or because I've stayed up late writing the past few nights and still feel the dregs of weariness?

One thing I'm learning: Grief strikes most ruthlessly when I am physically or emotionally drained.

SATURDAY, MAY 8

Today we received notice from Forest Lawn that the memorial tablet for Misty is in place. We're startled, surprised. We didn't expect it to be ready until July. I sit and stare at the formal announcement and think, *So. It is completed. We have done the final thing we can do for Misty.*

I weep.

Later: Reflecting.

I marvel over the sneaky ways of grief. Before Misty, I would have assumed that the process of mourning could be compared to being tossed into a deep pit.

It would be blackest at the bottom, but as one slowly, laboriously made his way out of the abyss, each step upward would be a little brighter, a little easier, until at last, with much effort, one would walk again in the sunlight, the darkness of the pit behind him.

It's not that way. I find I generally walk a level path, with a good grip on my emotions. But then, without warning, I trip and plunge headlong into the pit. The pain seeps into me like a clammy underground chill, paralyzing me with its iciness. I feel the impact of loss as if it were the initial encounter, as if I were accommodating afresh the first bitter knowledge of Misty's death.

Why is it this way? Why can I go for days or weeks without tears, only to be unnerved by the sight of a pregnant woman or a newborn baby? Why do I have "weepy" days in which everything reminds me of Misty and I cry at the slightest provocation? Why must grief be so cunning, skulking about, waiting in ambush, then cruelly attacking when I am most vulnerable or fatigued?

Tomorrow—Mother's Day—we will go to the cemetery to see Misty's plaque. I dread tomorrow. I don't want to hear sentimental talk about mothers and babies. Is there some way I can skip Mother's Day and go directly to Monday?

SUNDAY, MAY 9

Mother's day shortly after midnight.

Bill and I have just gone to bed. In the dark he reaches over and embraces me, and says, "Thank you for giving me three wonderful children."

His words caress and prick me at once. I begin to weep silently.

"What's the matter?" he asks.

I answer, "I'm thinking about the one I *couldn't* give you."

He gives me a special squeeze as if to say, *It's all right. I understand.*

We lie in silence for a few moments. Then I ask, "Do you think of her often?"

"Yes," he says, his voice catching slightly. "Mostly I think of her in heaven with my mother, who always loved children. And I think how happy Misty is with Jesus."

I think about that too.

Especially this Mother's Day afternoon when Bill and I visit the cemetery. As we stand close together in the cold wind beside Misty's grave, I study her new bronze marker graced with frolicking lambs and rabbits. The inscription reads:

MISTY LYNNE PAGE
JANUARY 7, 1982
OUR MOMENTARY CHILD
SAFE IN THE ARMS OF JESUS

I think: *Misty, our little momentary child, you're not here. Not here at all. As your daddy said, you're in heaven. We can't be near you by standing at your grave; we can only be close to you when we're close to Jesus.*

As the brisk wind whips around us, I wonder what Misty is like now with her perfect body and perfect mind. Would we know her? We hardly knew her before—just two brief hours together. Such slim memories, as fragile as the touch of gauze, as flimsy as gossamer on grass.

Of course, I remember Misty in a way that Bill cannot. I remember the unseen child I carried. I recall how she felt moving inside me—the solid, physical reality of her presence, the pleasant company she was in the silent hours of the night. I loved sitting in church and feeling her wiggle and kick. It was as if she were putting on a private show just for me. Even when I was surrounded by people, only I knew the antics and acrobatics going on undercover, how Misty swam and tumbled in her secret sea.

Sometimes I miss being pregnant more than I can say. How I regret that I can never attempt another pregnancy.

I've tried to analyze these feelings, and I've concluded there's a mystique about being pregnant. There is a secret savoring that has little to do with the finished product of a crying, wetting, demanding infant. There is the covert conspiracy of creation—the quiet, enduring knowledge that a miracle is encapsuled within your body, that a marvelous, inexplicable process has taken charge, and that no matter what else may occupy your days and weeks and months, all pales in comparison with that intricate unfolding in your womb. You feel special—a chosen vessel, a small replica of Mary who carried Christ Himself beneath her breast.

That sense of being honored, of partaking in a partnership of creation with the God of the universe, is reward in itself. It is enough to spark joy beyond words, that private ecstasy of the heart that I miss and yearn, against reason, to know again.

Father, in remembering what I have not, let me not forget what I have. Daily I learn anew that the losses make the gains all the greater, the minuses underscore the pluses . . . And what would sunlight be without night's stark contrast?

How grateful I am for my four children—for Misty who already sings heaven's praises, and for my three precious ones this side of glory, Your three inestimable gifts I still hold in my hand. I thank You even for the sorrow of a mother's heart, for where pain has carved its abrasions, there tenderness and gratitude can thrive. Thank You, Jesus, for this Mother's Day.

FRIDAY, MAY 28

THE NEWSPAPERS ARE FILLED with articles about the seventeen thousand aborted fetuses found in a large steel cargo container in Woodland Hills in February. I have a hard time reading the accounts. I'm stunned, sickened with incredulity and a crawling abhorrence. It goes beyond words, this instinctive revulsion I feel over babies deliberately mutilated and destroyed.

I can't stop thinking about the women—those seventeen thousand mothers who allowed someone to rip out their offspring, flesh of their flesh, those tender miracles—tiny, precious, unkept promises. Are we so vastly different that those mothers could cast away like trash what I strived so desperately to save? What has happened to the mother-hearts? Have they all been stilled, anesthetized?

What tipped the scales toward death?

Was it illegitimacy? Inconvenience? Poverty? Selfishness? Mere whim?

I cannot comprehend it.

I know what it means to lose a child—the enormity of loss that settles like dark, clinging soot over every aspect of one's life. Nothing is ever quite the same again. I know the hollow feel of an empty womb, the recurring ache of wondering what might have been. For as long as I live I will carry the image of an infant—ill-formed, unfinished, almond-eyed, with long tapered fingers and wet black curls, whose rosebud mouth sucked hungrily for life—the child Bill and I would have died to save.

But at least we glimpsed the miracle—the gift that defies earthly parameters and dwarfs human comprehension—the chance to participate with God in creating a unique individual with an eternal destiny, someone who will live as long as God lives.

I wonder: Have these women who forfeited their babies ever glimpsed the miracle? Do they know anything of loss? Do they grieve secretly in the dead silence of night? Does it ever come back to haunt them—the specter of a child who was and then was not? Do they have any idea what they've done?

A chilling, mind-numbing statistic: A million babies are slaughtered every year on the altar of convenience, of selfishness, of desperation, in the name of privacy and freedom of choice.

Oh, God, You who see the sparrow fall—can You hear the lingering echoes of a million tiny heartbeats snuffed to silence?

I can't think in terms of a million lives snuffed out.

I can think of only one child.

Mine.

My God, how can I absorb the reality of a million slain innocents when I cannot yet bear the loss of one tiny, damaged infant I loved?

Dear Lord, I cannot speak of this—I cannot think—cannot dwell on it. Rage spills out of me—mute, blood-red fury. I could shriek and rant like a shrew, an insane woman, but the sheer immensity of the horror strikes me dumb.

If I could speak—

If I could tell them—

If I could make them see the miracle—

If I could seize them by the shoulders and shake them—

If I could hold them and weep with them, these women who choose abortion—

But I can't.

At the moment my own wound is too raw. I can only scream out to these women in the silence of my heart, "How I wish your child had been mine!"

MONDAY, JUNE 7

I'M PACKING FOR FOUR DAYS OF teaching at Forest Home's School of Christian Writing in the San Bernardino Mountains. I can't help remembering the speech I gave there last year at this time on writing from one's passions. I said, "To write from your passions you must know what you love, hate, and fear the most." I confessed my own greatest fear: the loss of a child.

That very week Misty was conceived.

TUESDAY, JUNE 8

DURING THE NOON LUNCHEON at Forest Home, I sit with Dr. Bob Wells, an obstetrician at Long Beach Memorial Medical Center. Bob is acquainted with both my physicians, Dr. Anzaldo and Dr. Natter.

Bob and I become engrossed in a lengthy conversation about everything from childbirth and babies to abortion and genetic anomalies. I tell him about Misty. I sense his caring. I find it remarkably healing to talk with an obstetrician on a friend-to-friend basis. It's such a contrast to the usual formal, intimidating patient-to-doctor exchange.

I praise God for bringing Bob Wells to this conference for what I consider a divine appointment. It's as if a need I hadn't even recognized has been satisfied, a deep inner thirst quenched.

Evening: I'm to give the after-dinner speech. I commit to Christ my clammy hands and dry mouth and claim His love and power, plus a sound mind and steady voice. I feel His strength girding me even as I walk to the podium. I have things on my heart I need to share.

I talk about commitment, character development, and excellence in writing. I also talk about Misty. I speak about the need for us as writers—and as human beings—to be vulnerable and willing to expose ourselves emotionally to reach the brokenhearted and walking wounded of this world.

Afterward, the response is affirming. Several women tell me confidentially of the baby—or babies—they have lost. Another woman confides, "Most of us don't know what to say to someone who's lost a child. We feel awkward and maybe even a little guilty because our own kids are healthy and alive. We can't say we know how they feel, because we don't, and they know we don't. So what do we say to a grieving parent?"

I answer simply, "Just tell them, 'You are loved.' That's the most powerful message—and the most comforting—that one human being can communicate to another. It works when nothing else will."

WEDNESDAY, JUNE 9

My third day at forest home: I've agreed—perhaps foolheartedly—to be the subject of an interview in Millie Tengbom's class on interviewing. Millie, who lost her own first two babies, asked me in advance if I'd be willing to talk about Misty. With much trepidation, I agreed. Now here I am, my head on the cutting block. Still, even now, facing six interrogators, I feel this overwhelming compulsion to share my grief and explain what it's like to lose a child.

Amazingly, I'm able to talk calmly and openly about every aspect of my complicated pregnancy, Misty's traumatic birth and death, and how our family faced the crisis.

Some of the questions are as probing as a dentist's drill:

"Were you angry at God?"

"Not consciously," I reply. "But I was clearly angry at other, seemingly unrelated things."

"What things?"

I tell about being angry with Bill before the funeral and my fury over the rejected manuscript shortly after Misty's death.

"What did Misty look like?" someone else asks.

"How are you preventing another pregnancy?"

"What if you conceived another child like Misty—would you consider abortion?"

Hard questions. They keep coming for two solid hours.

Afterward I feel drained. But, oddly, I'm the only one in the room without tears.

THURSDAY, JUNE 10

I RETURN TO MILLIE'S CLASS TO hear the articles her students wrote based on our interview. Somehow listening to my feelings and experiences put down in other people's words is more painful than the original interview. I don't understand it. Can't articulate it. Perhaps it's because they've managed to capture a fresh glimpse, a vivid portrait of my grief, at once stark and palpable.

When the session ends, several people tell me how courageous I've been to share so candidly and expose myself to such vigorous interrogation. But I don't feel brave. I feel spent, unnerved, as if I've been through a ritual of cleansing.

And—madness or not—I'd do it all over again.

FRIDAY, JUNE 11

I'VE COME DOWN FROM THE MOUNTAIN—but not without paying a price. I'm home from the writers' conference, and my spirits have plummeted. I'm unbearably depressed. I face a cluttered house, loads of dirty laundry, and a fussy, demanding toddler. (Is this the same child who didn't give the baby-sitter a moment of trouble?)

When Bill comes home for lunch, we argue about

money—a stupid disagreement over a few dollars. Throughout the afternoon I cry and struggle with a blitz of conflicting feelings, even fleeting resentment over the barrage of piercing questions flung at me in the interview class at Forest Home.

In tears I ask myself: Where is that high spiritual and emotional plateau I trekked in the mountains? Where have all the loving, generous feelings gone? What happened to the joy?

I can't comprehend it. Why should those days of sharing Misty bother me now when they didn't bother me then? Why is the accumulated pain of four days crushing me now? Does a spiritual high always have to be followed by a spiritual low?

I wonder: Was Jesus ever plagued by such a reaction after ministering to the throngs? Is my reaction sinful—or just human? I feel so wretched right now. Do I need to confess it as sin?

Oh, Jesus, I'm thinking a lot right now about Your humanity. I know You are God, but I need to dwell on Your humanness for a while. I need to remember that Your earthly life wasn't easy for You. Even though You are Sovereign of the Universe, You made Yourself vulnerable to all the pain and anguish a human being can suffer. You didn't take living in Your stride. You felt it all—loss, rejection, disappointment, loneliness, exhaustion, hunger. Sometimes I forget that.

This past week as I shared my grief over Misty and opened myself to the hurts of others, I felt blessed. I praised You for using me to touch people's lives in a way I couldn't have before.

But, Lord, today I've come down from the mountain and I'm empty. The joy is gone, the blessing has fled. I can't look as charitably on those who, in all good faith, extracted from me my privacy and pain. I girded myself for their probing; I gathered in Your strength to meet their questions with love. And yes, I did love them. How warmed I was by their sincere expressions of caring.

But today I see that being vulnerable exacts a toll. The pain has washed in again like slanting rain on freshly plowed earth. The scar is still fresh, the wound still tender to the touch.

Is that how it was for You, my Jesus? Is that why You spent forty days alone in the wilderness with Your Father? Did it take that long to renew Yourself before You could open Your arms again to a beleaguered humanity?

Did the hurts and needs of people exhaust You physically and emotionally? Did it break Your heart to expose Yourself, holy God, to the uncomprehending throng? Did You feel alone in Your pain?

Is that why You sweat great drops of blood in the garden? Is that why, on the cross, with the sum total of my sins on Your shoulders, You cried, "My God, my God, why hast Thou forsaken Me?"

Lord Jesus, I know I can't begin to compare my pain with Yours. Mine is so slight in light of what You suffered. But it helps me, Lord, to recall that You were human too, and that You hurt. Man of Sorrows, thank You for living that name.

TUESDAY, JUNE 29

THE DOCTOR SAYS BILL MUST HAVE major surgery—a painful operation that will require about a month away from work. For the next few weeks Bill must also endure a strict diet of rice, tea, and eggs. He's decided to postpone the surgery until after the Christian Booksellers Convention in July.

We're both upset about this sudden turn of events. Just when life was starting to feel normal again!

SUNDAY, JULY 18

AT 9 A.M. BILL, HEATHER, AND I fly to Dallas for the Christian Booksellers International Convention. How I've looked forward to this week! Bill's as elated as I am. We both thrive on these annual work-vacations we spend with editors, publishers, and booksellers from around the world.

Ah, the spirit, the excitement, the hoopla—part circus, part tent meeting, a delicious melding of the spiritual and the commercial. Bill and I crave these days to recharge our energies.

THURSDAY, JULY 22

WHAT A WEEK!—CONCERTS, receptions, dinner with author Dorothy Martin, informal meetings with editors, an interview by *Christian Bookseller* magazine, and an autograph party with Moody Press, featuring my new teen novel, *Heather's Choice.* I'm in my element this week, my spirits soaring. How vivid and bright are these pleasures after that long, black tunnel of mourning!

Now: Bill and I board separate planes. He flies back to California to return to work, while Heather and I head for my parents' home in Michigan. A sweet, brief return to my roots before winging my way to Minneapolis for the *Decision* School of Christian Writing.

SATURDAY, JULY 24

Home again
in the house where I grew up—
summer sun caressing,
breeze deliciously cool,
stereo softly playing
yesterday's sweet and lazy love songs.
A neighbor burns leaves in his backyard—
hot pungent smell curling through screened
    windows,

mixing with wafting aromas of crisp brown
   chicken
baking in Mother's oven.
Daddy is working in the yard—
piddlin' as he calls it—
his handsome face sunburned,
dark wavy hair silver-streaked with years.
I see him from here
where I'm lying
on my parents' bed
resting
while Heather naps.
I'm home again
after a long painful year,
home again
to relax
and feel free
for a few fleeting days:
my mother's daughter,
my father's little girl,
but more so
me myself
still a long distance from them
my parents.
I'm not the child they raised.
I've walked too many miles
since those tender days.
Here
in these familiar rooms
memories of childhood
fragile as handblown glass
are easier to glimpse.
They glint with pieces of my past,
slivers etched with rainbow
reflecting sheer contrasting images
mirroring my separate selves
then and now.
Here I reflect remotely on Misty

without the pain.
Misty and pain
no longer synonymous.
I feel all right,
whole again,
and right this moment
pleasantly at home.

MONDAY, JULY 26

BILL TELEPHONES FROM CALIFORNIA. He's lonesome with the kids away at a Christian summer camp this week. "I miss you," he says wistfully.

"I miss you too."

"I've been thinking a lot about Misty," he adds with a sadness I've rarely heard in his voice.

His words pierce me like a dart. I've been so busy this past week that I've thought only superficially about Misty. But the quiet anguish in Bill's tone brings the reality of her abbreviated life and death back with a sharp twinge.

I'm touched by his feelings, in a strange way even pleased by them, for through all these months since January he has remained stoically silent about Misty. But now, as I hear the hurt in his voice, I think, *If he's going to cry I want to be there.*

I've never seen him cry over Misty.

Why do I feel so strongly that I need to see him cry?

Our conversation falters, a poor substitute for the intimacy we both crave. I yearn to reach out across the miles and embrace him, ease his loneliness, be there for him. But all I can say is, "I love you and miss you . . . and I think of Misty too."

TUESDAY, JULY 27

I'M BOTHERED. PERPLEXED.

Except for Mother, my family here in Michigan has

said nothing about Misty. Not a single word. It's as if by ignoring the matter the slate can be wiped clean, as if the past never happened. Why must everyone step so timidly around the subjects of death and grief? Do they assume it takes so little to erase so much? Do they think it doesn't matter anymore? That it's all forgotten?

I want to shout at them, "I had a baby and she died! What do you have to say about that?"

But I say nothing. I play their little game. Surely I wouldn't want to make anyone "uncomfortable."

But if I could summon the courage, I'd say to them, "You hurt me by your silence. Don't you realize I feel better when I talk about my baby? I feel a small measure of comfort when people admit that she existed, that she still exists, and that her earthly life, however short, had significance. I can't pretend she never lived or that she wasn't a crucial part of my life. I don't want you to pretend either. Don't you see? Your silence shuts the door on me. I can't talk freely; I can't talk at all. And if I can't talk to you—the people I love—who can I talk to?"

WEDNESDAY, JULY 28

I'VE NOTICED AN INTERESTING phenomenon taking place within my family. Since Misty's death my brother Steve and his wife June—after eighteen years of a childless marriage—have begun proceedings to adopt a Korean orphan baby; Bill's youthful, vivacious sister Annette, who'll soon be three times a grandmother, has applied to adopt a young child; in two months her daughter Karen will deliver her third child; and of course my sister Susi, after four years of barrenness, is expecting her first baby three months from now.

I feel profoundly touched that all of my brothers and sisters and my only niece are presently opening their arms to a new child.

I must admit that lately I've considered opening

my own arms to another youngster. Bill and I have talked at length about adopting a child. I feel such a strong emotional need for that "fourth child" for whom we have already made space in our hearts and lives. In fact, we've thought about adopting an Hispanic baby or even a special-needs child.

But I've come to realize I'm considering adoption for all the wrong reasons. I want someone to replace Misty—a baby to fill the empty places in my life. Until I can be sure I'm ready to meet a child's needs rather than having a child to meet my needs, I can't seriously think about adoption.

SUNDAY, AUGUST 1

I FLY TO MINNEAPOLIS FOR THE *Decision* School of Christian Writing. I'm excited, elated to be on the faculty with such prestigious names in Christian publishing as Joe Bayly, Sherwood Wirt, and Norm Rohrer.

Dinner with Luci Shaw, Margaret Anderson, Lois Johnson. What a treat!

An incredible week ahead.

I try not to notice that my arms already ache for Heather, back home in Michigan with my parents—her special Grandma Millie and Grandpa Giftie.

WEDNESDAY, AUGUST 4

A GLORIOUS WEEK! BUSY TEACHING an intensive, week-long fiction class and leading in-depth critique sessions with my students. Renewing old friendships with Sally Stuart, Margaret Anderson, Virginia Muir, others. Had lunch with Woody and Winnie Wirt, sat on a fiction panel with Joe Bayly, listened to Luci Shaw read her delightful poetry, joined in an anniversary celebration for Norm Rohrer.

Something I've noticed: At the Forest Home school in June I was preoccupied with thoughts of Misty. But this week I find myself thinking more of Heather. How I miss her. How she sings and dances and plays in the secret places of my heart!

THURSDAY, AUGUST 5

MISTY IN MY MIND AGAIN.

I talk at length with Norma Haist, a conferee who suffered two stillbirths—her first child and her fifth. Norma has written a book on grief which she is discussing this week with publishers. She shares it with me, and I, in turn, give her my journal to read. We both weep freely.

In talking with Norma I am reminded once again that people who mourn speak the same language. Those who have never suffered a profound loss know grief only as one recognizes an enemy on the street and knows instinctively to run. Most people can conceptualize some of the terror and panic that grief generates, but they don't know it as a daily soulmate; they aren't acquainted with grief's nuances, its habits, its idiosyncrasies, its persistence, its power.

Norma knows.

And so do I.

FRIDAY, AUGUST 6

NOON: THE *DECISION* SCHOOL ENDS. Lunch with editor Nathan Unseth, a personal tour of the extraordinary Bethany Fellowship facilities, then an evening flight back to Detroit.

The most exhausting leg of my journey still faces me—a sixty-mile ride from Metropolitan Airport to Jackson's Greyhound Depot on a grinding, loose-jointed, bump-jumping bus. I take the only seat, next to an old man who smells bad. We chat briefly, then retreat into our private thoughts. I gaze around from my cramped quarters at the most fascinating variety of rag-tag humanity I've seen in years.

The bus rumbles through every one-stoplight town and stops at every greasy, two-bit depot. I stare out the window at the immensity of dark countryside and the friendly lights of quaint towns. I talk silently with Jesus against a background cacophony of jive-talking dudes, profanity-spewing rowdies, crying babies, rock-blaring transistor radios, and the monotonous din of a dozen separate, muted conversations.

Daddy picks me up at the depot. I'm so glad to see him, so glad to be home. I hug Mother, then go straight to Heather's room. I walk in just as she is rolling off the edge of the bed. I rush over and catch her in my arms. She wakes and looks up at me with wide, startled eyes. I hug her until I'm afraid she'll break. How good she feels in my arms again!

MONDAY, AUGUST 9

I RETURNED HOME TO CALIFORNIA yesterday. Now I'm trying to settle back in—unpacking, washing clothes, sorting mail, cleaning house. Everything's a mess. I'm trying to bring back some routine amid the chaos before Bill checks into the hospital for his surgery next Monday—just one week from today.

Then Susi telephones with disturbing news: Her doctor is concerned that her placenta may be covering the cervix—a condition that would require a C-section. He's scheduled her for an ultrasound next Monday.

Oh, God, please don't let anything go wrong with Susi's pregnancy!

FRIDAY, AUGUST 13

AT NOON WE LEARN THAT OUR niece Karen, eight months pregnant, has postponed her scheduled weekend cruise on the luxury liner *S.S. Azure Seas*. Her cabin is available at great savings to us if we want to take it. Bill's sister Annette even offers to keep Heather for us. Only one problem: The ship sails tonight at 8 P.M. Do we want to go? Yes! How can we resist?

I spend the afternoon washing clothes and throwing things into suitcases (didn't I just unpack?). It's a mad scramble, but we're ready to go when Bill arrives home from work. But as he runs a few final errands, the gearshift on our car simply falls out of the steering mechanism. We endure a few tense moments while he repairs it.

Breathlessly, we board our ship at the Los Angeles harbor less than an hour before sailing. Russ and Annette see us off, standing on the dock as we set sail. Russ holds Heather up high in his arms so she can wave good-bye.

As our ship ebbs slowly away from shore, I watch Heather grow smaller and smaller, until finally I can no longer spot her little red jeans in the crowd. One of my last clear glimpses is of Heather screaming and clutching Russ as the ship's horn bellows mercilessly.

How I want to reach out and comfort her, but I can't. The ocean lies between us. It strikes me suddenly that I'm experiencing a very graphic parable of what death is.

I realize . . . I'm not good at handling good-byes anymore.

SATURDAY, AUGUST 14

THE *AZURE SEAS* DOCKS IN Ensenada. We disembark and watch rustic fishing boats unload mountains of anchovies—millions of tiny silver, slivery glimmerings. Gulls and pelicans circle and swoop, greedily devouring great mouthfuls of the tiny shimmering fish. One friendly pelican lands beside us and allows us to take our picture with him.

We walk gingerly along the pier where craggy, ruddy-faced, leather-skinned fishermen are mending enormous nets. The salty, pungent odors of fish and sea hang heavily in the air and settle in our nostrils. We walk for hours up and down the streets of Ensenada, visiting countless cramped, colorful shops bulging with handmade crafts, sculpted onyx, serapes and blankets, and garish animal pinatas. We watch street vendors wheeling their carts of fresh fruits and tamales, while tiny, dark-eyed children surround us, their eager hands outstretched, offering crepe-paper flowers for a quarter.

At sunset we return to the ship, our feet aching as we trek over the last half-mile of dusty road. Our arms are laden with trinkets and treasures—onyx cups, an ironwood quail, handblown glass unicorns. In spite of our weariness, our spirits are buoyed.

SUNDAY, AUGUST 15

ANOTHER TERRIFIC DAY. THE SHIP'S staff treat us like royalty; we shamelessly gorge ourselves on succulent foods—prime rib, steak and lobster, baked Alaska, fresh fruits, and fancy pastries. I savor the luxury of dining with silver, linen, and fine china instead of my usual Melmac, and of having fresh-cut flowers on the table and strolling mariachis to serenade us. As if this isn't enough, after dinner Mexican troubadours and colorful folkloric dancers entertain us.

Late in the evening, Bill and I sit together in a cozy corner of the piano lounge, relaxing, talking quietly, holding hands like young lovers. I study his features in the rosy lamplight. He has a strong face, ruggedly handsome with his full, gray-flecked beard. I love the solid, masculine strength of his features. I love being together like this, happy, comfortable with each other, our cares forgotten.

We need more times like this, I reflect silently. *Time alone to nurture our relationship, time to invest in romance, to enjoy each other. Time to be lovers again. There is so much between us that we haven't even tapped.*

Later, in the midnight stillness, I lie in my narrow berth and feel myself wafted to sleep by the gently rolling sea. Silently I thank God for this wonderful, unexpected weekend. I thank Him, too, for the sense of emotional stability and perspective I've regained these past few weeks. I realize something significant: During the entire cruise I haven't mentioned Misty to anyone. Not once. More important, the thought hasn't even occurred to me. Imagine. For the first time I haven't felt the need to talk about her.

Lord, I'm getting better.

MONDAY, AUGUST 16

OUR SHIP DOCKS JUST AS THE SUN rises gloriously over San Pedro. We disembark, check through Customs, and arrive home by 11 A.M.

At 3 P.M. Bill checks into St. Mary's Hospital for his surgery tomorrow. Talk about coming back to the real world! The starlight and romance of last night fades in the harsh glare of hospital walls. It is too sudden, too jarring. How can I fill out myriad hospital forms for Bill when my head is still dancing with mariachi music and romance?

But tonight reality settles gloomily over me. I sleep alone, praying in the gray silence of the night for Bill.

Take care of him, Lord. You know how much I need him.

And I pray for myself.

Please keep in mind, Jesus, that I'm just getting back up on my own wobbly legs. Please don't demand too much too soon, lest I fall flat on my face like an awkward, senseless, just-born calf.

TUESDAY, AUGUST 17

I DRIVE THROUGH MILES OF rolling predawn fog to St. Mary's Hospital in Long Beach. I can scarcely see the road ahead. I feel as if I'm traveling in a silent, vaporous nether world or suspended in limbo. Harrowing, this sensation. Am I moving? Heading in the right direction? Or am I following the swirling mists into some eerie, loathsome realm, some dusky region of desolation?

I don't remember ever feeling so alone before, so cut off from the rest of the world. I need Bill here with me. He should be driving, navigating this murky freeway.

Thoughts of Bill consume me now. He faces surgery in an hour. Major surgery. He should be fine. Yes, just fine. But there are no guarantees. I learned that with Misty.

What if something happened to Bill? What if I lost him?

I take him for granted. I expect him always to be there for me, navigating our lives, keeping us on course.

I consider myself an independent person in many ways—creatively, intellectually, emotionally. Still, I recognize that Bill is my head. He manages the complex-

ities of our everyday life and handles the practical, necessary matters, like driving the car, balancing the budget, paying the bills. While my head is often in the
clouds, Bill's feet are always firmly on the ground. He
lets me dream, and when my dreams soar skyward like
colorful kites, he lets me go chase them; but he holds the
string, drawing me back where I belong when the
winds turn brisk and buffet me.

Oh, God, please bring Bill safely through the surgery.

Shortly, when I enter Bill's hospital room, I learn
that he has already been medicated. He looks groggy,
pale, and so, so vulnerable. I sit down on his bed, take
his hand, and tell him I love him. We pray together,
then talk quietly. I realize his mind is growing increasingly disoriented.

Then, with amazing clarity, he says, "I cried about
Misty this morning—for the first time since the night
she died."

I stare wordlessly at him.

"I pictured her little face and how bad she looked,"
he continues tremulously. "Then I thought of Heather
and how beautiful and capable she is." He pauses for a
long moment, then adds with a wan half-smile, "Maybe
I was crying for myself too, for having to face surgery."

"It always hits when we're most vulnerable," I tell
him. "And being in a hospital brings it all back too."

Bill squeezes my hand. "Remember when we were
in the X-ray waiting room yesterday? Remember the
little girl—?"

"The one about the same age Misty would have
been? Yes, I sat and watched her. I couldn't take my eyes
off her."

"I was watching her too," says Bill.

"I know. When our eyes met, I knew what you were thinking. I almost cried."

"I got choked up too," he says.

"I had to turn away," I confess. "I couldn't bear the look on your face. It said everything I was feeling."

We lapse into a contemplative silence, clasping hands, sharing our grief, feeling the pain together in a positive, bonding way. I sense that this is a rare, priceless, untested dimension of our relationship.

Suddenly it's 7:30. Nurses and orderlies come, moving briskly, and wheel Bill out the door, down to the operating room. Numbly I walk alone to the family waiting room. I sit and wait. I send up wordless, urgent petitions to God on Bill's behalf. I jot notes in this journal. I wait. And wait.

Nine A.M.

Bill's surgeon appears in the doorway and beckons me over. "Your husband's fine," he tells me in his clipped, straightforward manner. "He was rather active, so we had to give him extra anesthetic, but there's no problem. He'll be in recovery for a few hours."

I spend the rest of the day in Bill's hospital room, first waiting over three hours for him to be released from recovery, then sitting by his bed reading while he sleeps off the effects of the anesthesia. Even when at last he does awake, he's groggy and in much pain.

As evening comes on I leave the hospital, weary, empty, my thoughts fragmented. But I return home to another piece of distressing news: My mother is hemorrhaging and had to be rushed to the hospital. She must have an emergency hysterectomy tomorrow morning.

So, a brand-new threat: *What if something happens to my mother?*

It appears that God is constantly reminding me these days that I must find my security in nothing and no one but Him. With the two people I rely upon most—my husband and my mother—both temporarily incapacitated, I am reminded disconcertingly of their vulnerability, their mortality. I recognize once again that we human beings have nothing, no one save Christ. All else is loan . . . can be reclaimed at any time. No one else can be all things to me except Jesus.

Mother telephones me from her hospital bed. She sounds anxious, her silences saying more than her words. How I long to reach out to comfort her. I scour my mind for reassurances, but come up with little more than worn clichés: *Take care of yourself . . . my thoughts are with you . . . don't worry.*

As much as I love her, I can do nothing for her, just as I can do nothing to alleviate Bill's ordeal. I can do nothing . . . but pray.

Ultimately, during the crises of life, each of us is alone. No one else can reach all the way, touch to the heart, heal and relieve the aloneness. No one—except Christ.

Oh, my beloved Christ! You alone can reach within each one of us to soothe, restore, and fill the empty places. You can ease Bill's pain and calm Mother's anxieties and renew my spent energies. I believe. I trust You for our separate, desperate needs.

WEDNESDAY, AUGUST 18

THANK YOU, FATHER.

Mother came through her surgery well. Bill is feeling better today than he did yesterday. I am less tired, more able to cope. And Susi's doctor has good news too. The ultrasound revealed that her placenta has moved and the baby has turned head-down, ready for delivery.

My Jesus, these past two days I've had no one to provide human comfort, but I've gratefully found solace in Your arms.

FRIDAY, AUGUST 20

Morning: TODAY I BRING BILL home!

I drive to the hospital breathing a sigh of relief that this will be my last trip—I who detest driving and have the navigational sense of a blindfolded sheep.

But my relief is short-lived. A careless driver pulls out from a side street and plows right into me. The only damage is to my right front fender and my nerves. As the apologetic driver and I exchange insurance information, I find myself wishing I had been somewhere safe—like in an airplane thirty thousand feet up.

In spite of my unexpected delay, I still manage to have Bill home before noon. He's in pain, but so far it's not as bad as he feared.

SATURDAY, AUGUST 21

The heat is suffocating today; the humidity saps our strength. Bill is in agony, suffering excruciating pains from his surgery. Heather is cranky, into things all day and pushing our patience to the limit. I spend the day running between Bill and Heather, doling out pills and preparing sitz baths, washing diapers and retrieving Heather from potential dangers, while trying to keep up with meals and dishes and household chores. All I want to do is collapse somewhere, but I can't find a spot that's cool.

Help me, Father, to see You in these scores of daily trials and annoyances. Help me to see You in a cranky toddler, in a sick husband, in a careless driver, in a scorching, unrelenting day. Help me to see You in all that I do.

There is one bright spot today. Susi stops by for a visit. I haven't seen her since before I left for Dallas in July. She's very pregnant now, proudly, delightedly so. What glee she effuses in simply feeling the baby kick. "There it goes," she marvels. "Watch! Put your hand right there. Feel it?"

I take pleasure in her joy. I think to myself, She's doing all the things I used to do, feeling the very same way. I remember it all so vividly.

Then comes the question that stuns me momentarily.

Susi's voice carries an edge of excitement as she asks, "Carole, would you like to be with me in the Alternate Birth Center when my baby is born?"

The idea is startling, intriguing, tantalizing. "Yes," I tell her. "Yes, I'd love to be there."

"I've asked Dan's sister Kay to be with me too," she says. "Kay's a nurse. And you've had so much experience with childbirth. I figure the two of you will be more help to me at critical moments than Dan."

"He doesn't mind?"

"He knows how desperate I am." She smiles, apprehension written in her eyes, and adds, "I'll be in the birth center for only twelve hours, then we all go home—Dan, baby, and me." She pauses. "I don't know anything about caring for a newborn, Carole. I never baby-sat when I was a teenager. I wasn't even around your kids when they were little. I don't know the first thing. . . . I was just wondering—would you mind coming home with me?—you know—staying with me for a few days?"

I chuckle. "You mean, so I can teach you everything I know?"

"Something like that." Her voice catches. "Since

Mother can't be here . . . you're the next best person . . ."

Sudden emotion sweeps over me. Impulsively I reach over and give her an affectionate squeeze. *Big sis, little sis.* I've never felt so protective of her. "Sure, Susi," I say with feeling, "I'd be glad to come help with your baby."

Later: This day is winding down at last, still sweltering even as midnight approaches. I'm frazzled. Can't sleep. All the windows are open and still no breeze. Scribbling a few sentences in this journal.

I can't stop thinking about Susi and her baby and the Lord's timing. I wonder: What will God teach me as I share in the birth and care of Susi's baby? I who crumble inside at the glimpse of a newborn—how will I handle this? Will Susi's birth experience be a unique source of healing for me, a rare means of affirming life and joy? Or will it resurrect a pain I have nearly managed to bury?

I won't know the answers for another seven weeks . . . when Susi's baby is born.

FRIDAY, AUGUST 27

FOR THE PAST COUPLE OF DAYS I've felt a strong compulsion to get back to work on the three novels I was writing some nine months ago. The manuscripts have sat in my desk drawer in various stages of completion, like patient offspring, waiting.

Last night I took them out, scanned them briefly, and felt blissfully at home. My special children of the mind were not strangers to me as I had feared after the passage of so much time.

Now the characters are once again loose in my mind, chatting, mingling, tossing out wonderful bits of dialogue and information about themselves that send me running to the typewriter to capture the phrases and ideas before they evaporate. My creative juices are bubbling up and overflowing; my mental energies are running at full steam.

Now if only my physical strength will catch up and time will slip me an extra hour or two to write. As it stands now, I've caught a nasty head cold and I'm washing dishes and laundry until 10 or 11 every night (amazing, the soiled towels that accumulate when Bill must soak in the tub six to eight times a day!).

In spite of my weariness, I stay up till 4:30 A.M. writing the first chapter of a brand-new novel. The very act of creating new characters and story lines pumps me with an energy that not even rest and sleep can provide.

Lord Jesus, I know You want me to write. I am most myself, most in tune with all I feel inside, and happiest, when I am writing. I pray that You will provide the time, the energy, and the inspiration. Let me write what pleases You, that which will reach and touch hearts so that they will see You more clearly. Thank You for restoring the urge to create, the deep, unshakable desire to capture those elusive butterfly wings called words to trace the universe and You and all of us.

SATURDAY, OCTOBER 2

THIS AFTERNOON I GIVE SUSI a baby shower. Hard for me to believe, but her baby is due next week, October 12.

Susi waddles and wheezes and looks as large as a helium balloon now that her usually svelte figure boasts an extra forty pounds. She is glowing and giddy as she opens her gifts. She laughs so hard during the games I fear she'll go into labor on the spot.

I bask in her joy. I feel no twinges when the dainty layettes, stretch suits, and infant sleepers are passed around. No attacks of self-pity. I hardly think about Misty.

Six months ago I couldn't have given this shower, or if I had, I would have seen tormenting parallels with Misty at every turn. I have come a greater distance than I realized. I've traversed new terrain. God keeps me at peace. I praise Him.

TUESDAY, OCTOBER 12

Susi's due date.

I telephone her, eager for news.

I'm disappointed. The doctor says nothing is happening yet.

"When are the pains going to come?" she asks as if she actually expects me to know.

SATURDAY, OCTOBER 16

Dan's sister kay telephones and says Susi is having intermittent contractions eighteen minutes to an hour and a half apart. And crampy feelings all day.

This could be it.

I have my suitcase packed and am trying to keep chores done so I'll leave a sane, organized household behind. A real challenge.

I'm washing diapers and dishes now; also typing the rough draft of my speech for the Santa Clara Valley Writers' Conference next Saturday.

But I keep thinking about Susi, wondering how long it will be. Four days late already.

God, give her an easy delivery and a healthy baby—please, Jesus!

SUNDAY, OCTOBER 17

Susi TELEPHONES, BREATHLESS with excitement. "Carole, my water just broke!"

"Oh, Susi—you're in labor?"

"I think so. Dan and I just finished dinner and were sitting on the sofa watching 'Sixty Minutes.' I got up to take the plates to the kitchen and suddenly I felt water running down my leg. I thought, *This is strange. What's happening here?* Then I knew."

"Are you leaving for the hospital now?"

"No. I called the birthing center. They said I don't need to come in tonight unless the contractions get bad. Otherwise I can wait till morning."

"You'll call me right away?"

"I'll call Kay. She'll call and tell you when she's going to pick you up."

"I'm ready now."

"Me too," Susi sighs. "It's going to be a long night."

"For all of us," I murmur.

MONDAY, OCTOBER 18

I GO TO A BIRTHING.

Today a promise will be fulfilled, a promise conceived the week Misty slipped into and out of this world so hastily. New life. A baby's cries and kicks, a baby whole and solid and perfect and wonderful. Susi's baby. Flesh of my flesh, once removed. My sister's child. We are all connected by love and blood, by generations past, a mutual heritage. My own little niece or nephew!

Kay and I arrive at the birthing center at 7 A.M. In a pleasant, homey room we find Susi sitting up in bed, looking eager and anxious at once. Dan's already pacing the floor with his "Let's get this show on the road" expression. The four of us greet one another as if we've gathered for a party. We have. A birthday party! Now it's simply a matter of waiting for the guest of honor.

Is everything ready? Yes, a tiny, lovely layette—soft kimono, fleecy receiving blanket, knit booties that would fit my thumb.

Kay, always jovial, teases, "Come on, Susi. I've waited long enough to be an aunt. When's that little baby coming?"

It can't be long now!

Or can it?

Susi labors, panting Lamaze-style. Dan times the contractions. The process goes on and on.

How soon? How soon?

The doctor comes in and checks her. He doesn't look pleased. "Nothing's happening," he announces. "You're not dilating. The cervix is still closed, tight as a drum."

We all heave a sigh of disappointment.

"We'll give it a little more time," the doctor continues, "and then . . ."

"Then what?" asks Susi.

"We may have to transfer you to the hospital for a C-section."

We all stare mutely at one another. We hadn't expected this.

The party . . . What happened to the party, the air of festivity, our celebration? We have come here to celebrate life and birth and joy. Now a shadow steals across our sun-washed room; the levity gives way to murmured concerns.

"I don't want a C-section," Susi murmurs. "I want to have my baby naturally."

Kay and I utter quick, earnest words of reassurance, but what can we really promise? Only that we will be here for Susi.

We wait, feeling helpless, while Susi labors on. We pray silently, watching the clock, timing her contractions. The minutes tick by. Surely something is happening now.

The doctor returns. Checks again. The same scowling expression. "No change," he says.

"What does it mean?" Susi asks.

The physician forms his words with care. "It means there's only a 10 percent chance that you'll deliver naturally." He pauses, draws in a breath. "And there's a 90 percent chance that by the end of the day we'll have to take the baby anyway. We can either do it now or wait till then."

"Do it now," says Dan.

"Wait till then," says Susi.

"I don't want you going through labor all day for nothing," Dan argues.

Susi counters, "But if there's even one chance to have the baby naturally, I've got to try for it."

"Okay," the doctor tells Susi. "We'll do it your way. But we'll have to move you over to the hospital . . . give you something to induce labor."

And so our little party disperses. A nurse helps Susi into a wheelchair and takes her across the street to the hospital. Kay, Dan, and I follow wordlessly and settle, disappointed, in the expectant fathers' waiting room.

A half-hour later: We enter Susi's room, find her hooked up to a fetal monitor. An intravenous needle drips pitocin into her arm.

The medication does its job. Within the hour Susi's contractions are coming fast and hard. She grips my hand, panting, the pain stark in her eyes. "The pains—they were nothing like this—before," she utters.

"That's good," I tell her. "That means they're accomplishing something."

But when the doctor examines her, he shakes his head and says, "Sorry, Susan. You're still not dilating."

Another hour passes. Dan paces, his nerves wire-tight. Finally Kay suggests they go get a bite to eat.

I stay with Susi, holding her hand, timing her contractions, uttering reassurances. It's as if the rest of the world has ebbed away, leaving the two of us alone to wage this arduous battle. I watch my sister—a woman in labor with her first child. I sit with her and watch and feel the contractions with her. I am in that bed heaving with the waves of pain. I imagine myself with child, summoning all my forces to expel it. I am my sister; we are one in a legacy of love. We knew the same womb, share a lifetime of memories, a universe of feelings we haven't even begun to explore.

I want to make things work for Susi, make the baby come. I want to taste and feel and breathe the wonder—my senses ring with the miracle of spilling out new bawling, breathing flesh.

Immerse me in life, oh, God. Wash away the taint of death.

Death?

Oh, God, no.

What if Susi's baby dies?

Have I brought a curse with me? Is it catching—this stigma of loss? *Oh, God, let Susi's baby be all right!*

A nurse brings Susi a Popsicle. She receives it like a grateful child. Her strength is waning. Still, she manages a smile. "The baby—he can't stay in there forever, can he?" she quips softly, patting her enormous tummy. "I mean, he—he's got to come out sometime."

Soon. *Please, God, soon.*

She's having a hard time riding the contractions now. The waves wash her under, leave her gasping. She gazes at me, manages to say, "There must be . . . some other way to do this, Carole. Let's go home . . . reschedule this event."

"Hang in there," I tell her soothingly, massaging her shoulder. "You're doing great."

She manages another faint smile and murmurs, "It's like someone's saying, 'Lights . . . camera . . . action. This is a take. We're not stopping for anything.' "

Three P.M. The doctor examines Susi again. "This kid's a yo-yo," he declares. "He hasn't dropped yet, so with every contraction he goes down, but afterward he pops right back up again."

"I'm trying," Susi moans. "I really am."

"Well, if nothing happens by 4, we'll have to go ahead and take him."

Susi gives an exhausted sigh. "Okay . . . it's fine with me."

Now, as the prospect of a cesarean section looms, new questions and worries surface. Suddenly Susi's not just having a baby; she's facing major surgery.

"I've never even been a hospital patient before," she frets.

Another concern: Will the doctor still allow Kay and me to be with Susi when the baby is delivered? It's not likely. Still, Susi asks. "Please, can Carole and Kay come in too? I need them with me."

And I need to be with Susi, as much for myself as for her. I've got to share in this birth. Oh, God, I've come this far. Don't let me miss it now!

The doctor is reluctant, but, apparently hearing the desperation in Susi's voice, he gives in.

Dan and Kay return from the hospital cafeteria in time to learn that the C-section is scheduled for 4. Dan has reservations about Kay and me being in the operating room, but Susi convinces him that she needs all the moral support she can get.

Now, finally, after long hours of waiting, it's time for action. Susi is wheeled to the operating room while Dan, Kay, and I dress in sterile masks and gowns. Suddenly we're giddy with excitement. Kay and I brandish our cameras like tourists on vacation.

The delivery room: A stark white room, bright lights, an awesome silence. Dan takes his place by Susi's head; Kay and I stand at the foot of the operating table, out of the way. We watch the surgeon make the initial incision.

133

I've never observed an operation before. I feel the adrenalin pumping, my heart pounding. Will I feel queasy? Faint at the sight of blood?

No. I'm fascinated.

With smooth precision the doctor cuts through each layer of skin. I see sudden bright, glistening red against the pale whiteness of Susi's abdomen. Deftly the doctor separates the folds of flesh and eases his hand inside, working something free. Then I see it: Incredible! A chubby white face with a squeezed-lemon expression. A person! Someone really in there! In an instant, expert hands lift out a plump, cheesy-white, wiggling body.

"It's a boy!" says the doctor.

Susi exclaims, "Praise the Lord, it's my boy! I knew it'd be a boy!"

Susi's baby boy cries lustily.

A nurse says, "He's a healthy eight pounds . . . and twenty-one inches long." Then she lays the baby beside Susi. Dan bends near. Susi utters tender mother-sounds and counts fingers and toes. I watch with joy, pure rapture. We are all hushed, as if standing on holy ground. I imagine the Nativity, blessed mother and child.

Thank You, Lord. Thank you, Susi. I've shared the miracle!

An hour later: Kay and I stand outside the nursery window watching Dan bend over the tiny isolette, holding hands with his naked new son, speaking father-sounds we cannot hear. We are as proud as any two aunts can be.

Evening: We see Susi at last. She looks exhausted, happy. Dan hovers beside her, beaming, every inch the proud papa. The four of us talk quietly, confidentially, Kay and I expressing our love, offering deep-felt congratulations.

Then a nurse bustles in and shoos Kay and me away, announcing, "The babies are coming to nurse!"

We linger, eager for a glimpse of our new little nephew. Jonathan Daniel is brought in, wrapped snugly in his cotton-soft blanket, his pink cherub face peeking out at us. I catch his newborn baby fragrance. I watch the nurse lay him gently in Susi's arms and guide his rosebud mouth to her breast.

Then the nurse abruptly draws the curtain between us.

It's over. The realization stuns me: I've walked with Susi as far as I can go.

I walk out swiftly, taking long strides down the maze of corridors to the hospital exit. *Run, go, escape!* A weight presses in my chest. I fight back tears. I feel incredibly empty, alone. What's wrong with me? Why this sudden, surging swell of emotion? There are no words for the cataclysm of anguish that floods me now.

Then, with a shattering jolt, I understand: I can share the birth . . . but I can't take home a baby.

TUESDAY, OCTOBER 19

I'M BACK TO STEP ONE.

Yesterday I rejoiced with Susi over the birth of her new baby.

Today I weep for myself. I weep for what might have been, for what will never be. I weep for Misty—a promise snuffed out, a cherished hope dashed nine months ago.

It could have been today, the way I feel now.

All day yesterday I heard the steady whooshing sound of Susi's baby's heartbeat on the fetal monitor. In my mind it was Misty's heartbeat, the pounding rhythm reminding me that she lived, actually lived inside me once. She existed. (Was I already forgetting her?)

And later, when the nurse brought in Susi's baby, sweet and new, wrapped in his receiving blanket, and laid him in her arms to nurse, I recalled vividly what I'd lost with Misty. This was the ritual, those first magical moments of communion between mother and child. But they were Susi's moments, not mine.

It's not my baby; it's Susi's.

And the pain is still there, in every pore, in every sensation, sweeping clear to the nerve-endings.

I want my baby. I can't have her. She's gone.

Susi has a baby now. I love Susi. But her baby's not my baby, even if I wish it were. He's not Misty. He's somebody else. Not a baby I recognize with mother-love. He's a stranger—a sweet, wonderful baby, but not mine.

Where is this child I love—the one who is missing, who has left a baby-shaped vacuum in my heart? I sense her presence. I know her by name. I feel profoundly the absence of all the rituals of growing and living and loving that should have been ours.

She is gone.

I had almost begun to feel that she never existed; a comforting blindfold covered my memory's eye.

But now I remember. I relive it all. I make comparisons. I torture myself by recounting every exquisitely painful detail in my mind.

Why do I have to go back to Square One?

Why do I have to start all over again to forget?

I thought I was so well-adjusted. I thought I was doing so well. Is the lesson of grief so hard to learn that I must repeatedly be sent back to the beginning like a dull schoolchild?

Lord,
I am learning how little I know
of the landscape of my soul.

FRIDAY, OCTOBER 29

THE TEMPEST IS PAST.

I'm on an even keel again.

I've just spent five days at Susi's home, keeping house, cooking meals, caring for her while she recovered from her surgery . . . and helping her care for baby Jonathan. Surprisingly, I felt very few pangs or yearnings as I held Jonathan or watched Susi nurse him. While I had a few uneasy moments at first, they weren't as bad as I had feared.

In fact, being with Susi this week had the peculiar effect of desensitizing me to newborn babies and to the lingering mystique of new motherhood. I needed this "overexposure" to a newborn infant, this "overdose" of maternal nuturing and its accompanying demands and exhaustion—the missed sleep and midnight feedings, the shrill, insistent baby cries, the foul odor of soiled diapers and curdled milk upchucked on freshly laundered clothes . . .

Amazingly, I can now appreciate Susi's baby for just who he is—my sweet little nephew—no more, no less. Jonathan Daniel is eight pounds of darling, grim-faced little old man. He is blond and fair, with deep blue eyes and the wisdom of the ages in his sober brows. I've never seen such a distinctive nose in a newborn—apparently a combined legacy from his father Dan, my brother Steve, and my Grandfather Curren.

Jonathan. The name means "Jehovah gave." It would have been Misty's name had she been a boy. But it belongs to Susi's baby now.

Jonathan Daniel Porter.

He is Susi's child.

And I am glad.

I realize I owe Susi and little Jonathan a debt of gratitude I can't begin to put into words. God has used them to bring me through the most traumatic phase of my grief over Misty. God allowed me to share with Susi some of the most intimate moments of her pregnancy and childbirth, and He allowed me to feel afresh my loss over Misty.

But I have survived. And I will continue to survive.

And I know in time I will thrive, because I am stronger than I ever could have been had Misty not lived and died.

I have glimpsed, with a brief, brilliant clarity, how God works all things for our good . . .

MONDAY, NOVEMBER 1

Strange . . . yet not so strange.

I'm finding it increasingly difficult to write in this journal. I want to write about something else, concentrate on other things.

I can hardly recall the person I was a year ago when I was placidly pregnant, never suspecting the problems that lay ahead. I don't want to dwell on the past anymore. Why should I keep replaying the memories? They only mushroom into great dark ogres that wreak havoc with my emotions.

Lately I feel as if it's too much effort to articulate my feelings. Why should I keep analyzing them, picking at them like pieces of lint on a dark suit? I'm tired of it.

Maybe I don't need this journal as much as I did before. Is it possible? Am I beginning to be free at last to move on to other interests, other projects?

I know this: I want to go work on my novel. And I don't want to miss any more of *now.*

SUNDAY, NOVEMBER 21

Bill and I participate in a panel on grief in our Sunday school class, sharing the platform with a young woman whose husband recently died, a man who lost his father, and a woman mourning the death of a close friend. One by one, we open ourselves to the scrutiny of a hundred people, frankly answering their questions about what it's like when someone you love dies.

Bill and I speak about Misty, confiding how it feels to lose a child, holding nothing back. Bill tells how it was for him; I tell how it was for me. This is one of the most candid, intimate moments of our lives, and we are sharing it with a roomful of acquaintances and strangers.

It's like standing naked before the world, laying bare our souls, exposing the hurt . . . and hoping they understand.

They do. They weep with us.

The connection we feel with one another is incredible; their compassion is nearly palpable. We feel immersed in love.

Afterward I'm exhausted, euphoric, exhilarated.

A paradox: I am spent; I am full. I have never felt so close to so many in a single incident of sharing.

One man, his voice heavy with emotion, tells me, "I'm in awe. I don't know what to say. The way you all opened your hearts and made yourselves so vulnerable, . . . I feel as if I'm standing on holy ground."

THURSDAY, DECEMBER 30

A DIFFICULT DAY FOR ME. One year ago Dr. Anzaldo told us there was no hope for our baby. I keep thinking about it all day. Feel weepy. As if it were all happening again . . . now!

Will it always be this way? Long stretches of peacefulness and calm punctuated by momentary deviations into emotional mayhem and madness?

Ah, Grief, you are preposterous, raving, heedless, quirky. You are a fire-breathing dragon, a buffoon, a maggot, a knight-errant stalking the land for bleeding hearts. You smell blood, taste it, and ferret out the wounded with fiendish glee.

Fickle Grief, you are wanton in your ways.

FRIDAY, JANUARY 7

LORD, IT'S BEEN A YEAR—not a day, not forever—one year since Misty. The pain strikes less frequently, its edge less cutting. But Misty remains part of me, a silent resident in my thoughts, the most tender spot in my soul. She colors everything I am, the way I look at the world, my responses, my motivations.

I will never again see a retarded youngster with the detachment I once had . . . for Misty could have been that child. I will never hear of a child's death without reliving Misty's fleeting hours on earth. I will always feel a wrenching heart-tug when I glimpse a newborn baby. I will never be able to talk about the issue of abortion without tears and a sense of outrage.

Since Misty, I am more vulnerable, more anxious over my other children's welfare. I overreact when Heather falls or when Kim and David are late from school. In a way, it's a loss of innocence. No longer do I feel insulated, protected from the tragedies of life—the impossible, the unthinkable. I know now that anything can happen. Yes, it can happen to *me*.

Some things I'm not.

I'm not depressed.

I'm not cast down.

I'm not floundering.

Since Misty, I savor life as if everything were new.

Last year our family was shaken to the core. We could have crumbled. Many grieving families do. I lost an essential piece of myself—my child, my flesh, a bright, beloved promise, part of the future.

I could have lost more—peace, purpose, pleasure in living.

I am stronger than I was, wiser, more appreciative. I have survived. Windblown and weather-beaten, still I stand. I can be genuinely happy, laugh wholeheartedly, delight in my other children, and love Bill again without thinking of our loss.

I feel almost normal. I am cheerful more than I am sad. God has never left me to walk alone. I am propelled by an energy honed by profound hurt.

Thank God, our family has not been scattered, or shattered, but gathered together. We possess more this year than last—grateful hearts, priceless routine days, commonplace joys, oneness as a family, and a sense of having narrowly escaped devastation.

God has blessed us. He is with us. For what more can I ask?

Misty, this is my only birthday gift for you—a love note from your mommy.

You would have been one year old today. (Does anyone remember?) I can't help but wonder how it would have been if you'd been born healthy and whole.

We would be celebrating a birthday today instead of mourning the first anniversary of your death. There would be a cake with one candle and a frilly dress and bright cards from loving relatives.

You would be a darling toddler, just starting to walk—clumsily but eagerly—and talk, with words only we, your parents, could understand. What a day of joy it would have been. We would have sung to you and kissed you and told you how happy we were to have you as part of our family.

But today *is* a special anniversary for you, Misty— a year since you slipped quietly through heaven's gates. Are the angels celebrating this precious day? Are they singing to you now? Is Jesus embracing you to remind you of His caring? Or don't you need reminding in the presence of His all-encompassing love?

I know. You don't need to mark dates and anniversaries. You are not bound by the strictures of time and space.

I try to imagine how it is for you, my child, but I

can't begin to comprehend your world. I know only that there is no dark to fear, for God is light; there is no pain to endure, no loneliness to suffer, for God Himself has wiped away your tears. He has given you all that I, your mother, could not—a perfect body, flawless love, a glorious home, eternal life.

Your celebration there is far grander than anything we could have given you here. For now we are worlds apart, separated by life and death, by time and eternity. We are the dying, you the living.

Recently your daddy told me, "Misty is more alive than we are. *We're* dying; she's not."

Someday we will celebrate your birthday together, little daughter. Until then, Misty, remember how much your daddy and I love you.

SATURDAY, MAY 21

My EXCITEMENT RIDES HIGH TODAY!

Bill, Susi, and I drive to the Los Angeles International Airport to meet our brand new little three-month-old niece, Lindsey Morgan Gift. She arrives at 1 P.M. on a flight from Seoul, Korea, with several other Korean orphans and their escorts from the Bethany International Adoption Agency. The children have a two-hour layover before flying on to their new families in Michigan and other states. As incredible as it seems, this very evening Lindsey will be placed in the arms of her new parents—my brother Steve and his wife June.

But at this moment—several hours before Steve and June will meet their new little daughter—we have the rare chance to see her first.

As the Korean youngsters and their escorts emerge from the plane, my eyes eagerly scan the round cherub faces.

Which one is Lindsey?

My gaze settles on the tiniest traveler—a beautiful,

bright-eyed infant with the porcelain-perfect face of a china doll. I fall instantly in love with her.

Lord, let her be the one, I pray silently.

Yes!—the escorts confirm it—this smiling baby with the coal-black hair and dark, almond eyes is little Lindsey. Even as I touch her soft, plump cheek and feel her tiny hand grip my finger, I imagine how Steve and June will feel when they take her in their arms.

I seal these precious moments with Lindsey in my memory. Already I feel a special bond with her, just as I felt with Susi's little Jonathan at his birth.

Yes, Lord, this, too, is a birth—the beginning of Lindsey's life in her new homeland with her American family—her amazing journey, not down the birth canal, but halfway around the globe.

I marvel. God has let me share the miracle again. Just as I saw Jonathan moments before Susi's first glimpse, so now I've seen my brother's baby daughter hours before she's placed in his arms.

TUESDAY, DECEMBER 27

SUMMER . . . AUTUMN . . . WINTER. The months have sped by. This journal that has fed my soul, caught my tears, heard my cry—its pages are empty now, uncharted.

I'm growing . . .

Misty . . . I've changed in the two years since your birth and death.

I celebrate life more now than I ever did before you touched me. I caress the commonplace with marveling fingers. How I savor precious moments with those I love!

In all my sadness there is a shining—a joy glimmering like the spangled froth of a moonlit ocean. No black holes anymore. No bottomless pits.

Likewise, in all my joy a wistfulness emerges; my pleasures are marbled by faint ripples of melancholy.

There are no pure, solitary feelings, no single-hued emotions.

Joy is sorrow, sorrow joy. My arms are full, my arms are empty. Sometimes I sleep with an old brown Teddy bear—I, a middle-aged child for a few absurd hours.

Can arms know there was something they were supposed to hold?

Someone?

SATURDAY, DECEMBER 1

ANOTHER YEAR HAS ROLLED BY.

Hard to imagine: Nearly three years since Misty.

Bill and I take our four-year-old Heather to Knott's Berry Farm, where she's captivated by Camp Snoopy and the costumed Charlie Brown and Lucy. Squealing with delight, Heather bear-hugs the burly white beagle, and how she laughs with glee when Lucy hugs her daddy!

We stroll through the rustic ghost town and linger in the petting zoo with its baby goats, ponies, and lambs. We ride the Western stagecoach, the merry-go-round, and the old-fashioned train with its steam locomotive.

In the recreation area Heather swings, seesaws, and climbs on the old log fence. I watch her playing alone, a solitary child.

Sometimes, whether we're at the amusement park, the playground, or the beach, I watch Heather and imagine *two* children frolicking together. A smaller, younger version of Heather tracing her steps, laughing merrily, romping in the sunshine. It seems so natural for there to be two.

It's a strange phenomenon . . . like the phantom pains of a missing limb. The limb, although physically severed and visibly absent, makes known its "presence" in ways that defy reality or reason. It's as if the missing arm or leg were still attached, one with the body. Muscles ache, fingers twitch, fists clench, toes cramp with pain.

> It's that way with losing a child.
> Phantom pains. Phantom child.
> Invisible, but still a part of me.
> A peek-a-boo presence
> slipping in and out of my imagination,
> playing hide-and-go-seek in my heart.
> Phantom child on the empty carousel horse,
> soaring in the empty swing,
> making sand castles on the desolate beach—
> her laughter riding the wind,
> her tears streaming in the rain.
> Sweet shadow-dancer.
> Flickering firefly.
> Gone.
> But still my child.

SUNDAY, OCTOBER 20

MY JOURNAL IS DUST-FLECKED lately, untouched, unread. I don't recall when I last wrote in it.

It's been almost four years since Misty.

Life has moved on steadily, inevitably away from our little daughter. Most of the time now Misty is only a passing thought, a poignant memory in my mind, a soft spot in my heart.

But at times, on days like today, I realize that the specter of *someone missing* hangs over us still.

Strangely, Heather—who was only one and a half when Misty came and went so swiftly—feels her absence most keenly. Heather is the only child in a house full of adults, and how she longs for a playmate her own age. Five years old now, Heather talks about her baby sister nearly every day, always praying for her at mealtime grace: "Dear God, take care of Misty and help her grow up. Please let me play with her when I get to heaven, and let me hold her and rock her . . ."

Words so innocent, so earnest, so wrenching.

Heather is not nearly as easy a child to raise as Kim and David were. They were as mild and genial in disposition as they were bright. And they were playmates for each other. Heather, growing up alone, is complex, intelligent, demanding, a contradiction of shyness and aggression, her temperament stubborn, shrewd, bubbly, explosive.

We clash all too often. And always there is the talk of her little sister, her undeniable yearning for that younger, tiny companion she never knew but profoundly misses.

Today—Sunday—things come to a head. Heather is ill, so she and I stay home while the rest of the family goes to church. We spend the hours relaxing together on her bed—she drawing and practicing her letters, I doodling cartoons for her and catching snatches of a novel I've wanted to read.

Just as I marvel over how smoothly the day is going—how even-tempered Heather is for a change— she challenges me. "I can skip rope with my blanket," she announces.

"No," I warn. "You'll fall down and hurt yourself."

"No, I won't!" she exclaims, jumping clumsily.

"If you hurt yourself, I won't feel sorry for you," I tell her. It's the wrong thing to say; I sense it immediately. I should simply force her to stop, but I know that will precipitate a blowup.

Not today, please, when things have been so pleasant.

She jumps, stumbles, hurts her knee, turns to me for comfort.

I offer none but continue reading, my jaw set resolutely.

She pushes for the expected consolation.

"I told you I wouldn't feel sorry for you," I remind her.

Now the blowup I tried to avoid—the screams, the protests, the heated demands for my sympathy. Why is it? Everything with her is a challenge, every incident a confrontation.

Refusing to listen to her tirade, I go to the bathroom and lock the door. Heather follows, pounds on the door with her fists, and swears loudly. The words—adult words of deep frustration—erupt with a bitter irony in her tender child's voice. I'm alarmed, dismayed. Where did she ever learn such words?

I throw open the door and stalk to my office for the ruler, intending to swat her bottom for cursing. I march her to her bedroom and sit down with her on the bed.

But seeing her desolation, I feel compelled to talk to her instead. I bend my face to hers, lift her quivering chin, and stare directly into her eyes. Already her eyes are wet, tears coursing down her cheeks, her expression crumbling.

"What are we going to do?" I ask. "I want us to love each other and be happy together, not angry and upset." We talk about obedience, about her minding Mommy and Daddy. My words come, artless and urgent; I don't know if they're the right ones or not, or whether they'll make any difference.

Heather cries harder, her sweet, round face broken in contrition. "I love you," she says.

"I love you too," I assure her, drawing her into my arms, rubbing her warm bare back under her shirt.

"I miss my little sister," she cries. "I want her here to play with me."

Always back to this—Misty, the missing member of our family, the absent little playmate.

"I know. I miss her too," I confess. "But all we have right now is each other, honey. You're the only little girl I've got."

147

Heather rears back and protests, "You've got Misty! She's in heaven, but she's still your little girl!"

The words break my heart. I begin to weep, pressing Heather's head against my chest, my tears wetting her hair. She strains away and stares up at me, her large, dark eyes registering dismay. Now she begins to sob in earnest, unable to cope with my tears. I hug her fiercely. We weep together, sharing these unexpected moments of grief.

Even now.

After almost four long years.

Most of the time I feel as if I've walked such a vast, untraceable distance from Misty, separating myself from her by myriad emotional miles. But at moments like this I realize I haven't moved far away at all.

Such is the paradox of grief.

WEDNESDAY, JANUARY 7

MISTY, YOU WOULD HAVE BEEN five years old today.

You are still on my mind and in my heart, even though we rarely visit the cemetery or place flowers on your grave anymore. In fact, this was the first Christmas that we didn't put a little decorated tree beside your bronze marker.

I don't remember when we last visited your grave.

I don't think of you being there. I won't limit you to that little plot of grass behind those iron gates.

Still, we would have visited the cemetery today on your fifth birthday, but your family is so busy these days. Your daddy works diligently as an aerospace engineer; your mommy is busy teaching and writing books. Your sister Kim is in college now and working part-time at a dress shop in the mall. Your brother David is in high school and working at Burger King. They're both honor students, juggling their free time between church activities and dates. And your sister Heather is a bright first-grader at Grace Christian School, and oh, she's already so eager to read books and write stories.

But as busy as we are, you are not forgotten, little daughter. Whenever someone asks your daddy how many children we have, he always says, "We have four children. One in heaven, and three living at home."

Misty, I think you would be proud of your family. We all love one another dearly. We're a happy family, blessed with so much.

For me, one of those blessings is my memory of you.

Misty, you have taught me as much as any of my other children—secrets of living and dying I never asked to know. But now, in retrospect, I'm grateful for those lessons. You see, I'm learning that it isn't the events of my life that matter, but my relationship with Christ *through* those events that spells joy or despair.

I've realized that what counts, too, is the meaning I ascribe to those events, how I *view* what happens to me. Can I see a purpose and a plan? A potential for good? Do I sense Someone greater than I walking me through the dark? And does the dark make God's presence all the more palpable, His touch all the more precious?

Yes!

Like a blind woman I have touched the face of God with desperate, groping fingers, and I have felt new planes and angles of His vast terrain. I have discovered a consummate beauty in my Savior I'd never glimpsed before. I have seen my Lord in a way I never could have known outside of grief.

So you see, my little daughter, I've learned that Christ doesn't waste any of our experiences. If we let Him, He turns even our heartaches to gold; He tempers us, makes us strong through our sorrows and disappointments. I'm glad I listened years ago when God spoke to my heart and said, *Be willing to have more children . . . I have much to teach you . . .* Yes. Oh, yes! He was so right.

Now, when I think of you, Misty, I remember you as one of the most positive experiences of my life—positive because of what Christ did in my heart, what He taught me, and the way He has used your daddy and me to touch other hurting lives.

Even the remnant grief that still strikes occasionally drives me back to the arms of God and reminds me of my humanity, my dependence on Christ, my need to show compassion to others.

Misty, you weren't here long enough to know about heartaches and sorrow, about sin and regrets. You never misbehaved or brought disappointment to your Heavenly Father or your earthly father. In fact, your daddy often says you're the only one of his children he never had to spank.

But, Misty, the world is full of broken people and broken hearts. Because I lost you, sweet child, I know how the wounded feel. But because of Christ, I know what it means to be healed.

And if I could, I would reach out to the hurting world and tell them, "The Great Comforter waits to gather you into His arms. You are loved. Oh, you are so loved!"

Now
at last
I'm closing the cover on this journal, Misty.
Inscribing the last word.
Setting this little volume aside.
It's time to go on to other things.
It doesn't mean that I'm forgetting you, child.
I never will.
Or loving you less.
Who can measure love that spans time and
    eternity?

REUNION

Someday when I'm old
and someone asks if I'm looking forward to
   heaven
I'll say I'm eager to see my Jesus
but there's someone else I want to see too.
I'll say
it's been thirty or forty years since I've seen her
and the time we spent together was all too
   brief—
an hour or two,
that's all,
and she was so tiny and frail
she spent that time just trying to breathe.
I never had a chance to find out who she was
or what she was like—
what she could have done,
what she could have been,
but she was my child,
flesh of my flesh,
my own,
and I love her
with limitless love.
My other children grew up
and grew older with me
but this one—
the one I'm longing to see—
stayed the same through the years—
her face fixed in my memory
like a faded snapshot,
its corners worn
from too much handling.
Through the years,
the good and bad times,
I've dreamed of that distant reunion
and imagined the moment

I could look her in the eyes
and say,
Darling,
your mother's missed you
but we'll never be apart again.